REVISED THIRD EDITION

FLEA MARKET
TRADER

Edited by Steve Quetermous

COLLECTOR BOOKS

P.O. BOX 3009

Paducah, Kentucky 42001

The current values in this book should be used only as a guide. They are not intended to set prices, which vary from one section of the country to another. Auction prices as well as dealer prices vary greatly and are affected by condition as well as demand. Neither the Author nor the Publisher assumes responsibility for any losses that might be incurred as a result of consulting this guide.

INTRODUCTION

Since the publication of the first two editions of *The Flea Market Trader* there have been changes in the collecting trends in this country. It seems more and more that there is a following for almost every item imaginable. As prices increase on a popular collectible, people "latch on" to a previously ignored item that is still reasonably priced.

Some collectibles apparently have reached their peak in popularity and prices have stabilized somewhat in these areas. Generally speaking, however, most everything has at least kept up with inflation and most items have surpassed it.

The flea market is stronger than ever in this country. It remains an excellent place for the serious collector or the "accumulator" to further his collection and broaden his knowledge of antiques. This revised edition is a look at some of the changes that have come upon the scene in the last couple of years. Many new categories have been added and previously existing categories have been streamlined and completely revised to give the collector a more balanced view of collecting and price trends.

Since much of this material has been taken from other books on collectibles, there is a comprehensive list of specific acknowledgements and credits that can be found in the back. A bibliography has been included for use by the collector wanting more in-depth information on the subjects included.

We've tried to stick to the same format, some brief introductory comments, a price listing, and some sample illustrations. In keeping with the guidelines of the previous editions, we've attempted to present a cross-section of the thousands of items found at nearly any large flea market across the country.

It would be impossible in a volume this size to list every item that would fit into a particular category. It is possible, however, to present a survey of a category with random items and selected illustrations to aid in identification. Illustrations have been picked that accurately represent the category. The collector is encouraged to further research any area of interest. The books used to compile this guide contain the work of some of the most well known collectors and writers in the antiques field.

FLEA MARKETS

Flea markets, swap meets and trade days are all names for the same general activity — collectors and dealers getting together to buy, sell or trade items of interest. The best time to find a bargain at one of these functions is very early — even as participants are unpacking. Many times, "good finds" will change hands among dealers several times, increasing in price with each change. An early buyer can avoid the inflated price by finding the item first. Always look for the first time exhibitor. His prices are generally lower and he is not always sure what sells best at flea markets.

Staying late can also prove profitable. Sellers will sometimes settle for less rather than pack an item and carry it home again. This is especially true of large and hard to transport pieces. Bargaining is a tradition at flea markets, so, never be afraid to offer less than an item is marked. But, always be willing to compromise.

The flea market is unique, in that it has something in every price range. Rare collectibles and cheap "what-nots" can all be found. It is still a good place to witness the changing price trends in the antique market. Prices are constantly changing as more collectors emerge and new collecting fads develop. Always watch for "sleepers", those overlooked items that suddenly become the hottest things on the market. The expert can be seen developing an extensive collection and at the same time, the novice can be seen enjoying a leisurely spent afternoon at the flea market.

BEWARE

As trends change and good merchandise appreciates in value, there are those that duplicate, repair, and misrepresent hard-to-find and valuable items. There will always be these "quick buck" artists. The best way to defend against them is by researching your field and becoming familiar with what is available. Always be careful, regardless of whether the deal you are making is for only a few dollars or several hundred. If you are not sure about the authenticity of an item, get an authoritative third opinion, or ignore it altogether. Always beware of "the good deal", you could be getting fleeced.

Besides the ever present "rip off artist" there is also another area to be careful of. Many companies re-issue and reproduce popular nostalgia items that find their way quickly to the selling tables. Though these items are not produced to fake the buyer they are many times presented as old or original collectibles. With the current trend toward nostalgia in this country there has been an upsurge in reissues and reproductions.

PRICING

Extensive research has gone into pricing this volume. Unless noted, the values are for pieces in excellent condition at the retail level. Dealers will, naturally, buy at lower prices in order to stay in business. Some areas of the country will have higher prices on some items and lower values on others, due to the availability and popularity in that area. Also keep in mind, that an item is worth as much as the buyer is willing to pay or as little as he is willing to pay — no more, no less.

If the collector disagrees with the price evaluations in this guide he is encouraged to do more research to ascertain a fair value for the merchandise in question. This book is not produced to provide a hard, fast rule on the absolute value of a particular item. It is instead intended to give a general comparative view of price trends at flea markets today.

This book is designed to aid the flea market frequenter, but its use is not restricted to him. It is also ideal for use by the garage sale shopper, antique collector, dealer and nostalgia lover. It is built for use. Don't be afraid to carry it along on buying trips. And, happy flea market trading!

CONTENTS

Advertising Buttons

Pinback buttons featuring products or manufacturers have been popular for a number of years. Because they are attractive, colorful, and deal with early advertising they are in demand among collectors. These buttons were offered as premiums to promote sales. Prices range from a few cents to several dollars on this item. The collector should act with caution when purchasing pinback buttons because many are being reproduced.

Aunt Jemima "I'se in town,
  honey" $3.00-5.00
7up "Freshup Freddie" . $2.50-3.50
Dr. Pepper, man in top
  hat $5.00-7.00
Pope Bicycles $6.00-8.50

Philip Morris, "Vote for
  Philip Morris" $3.00-5.00
Buick, "Everybody
  knows." $5.00-7.00
Pontiac, "Aims for
  Victory" $3.00-4.00
Fleischman's Yeast,
  doughboy $8.00-10.00
Oscar Mayer German
  Weiners $2.00-3.00
Gold Medal Flour, Washburn
  Crosby Co. $1.50-2.00
Montgomery Ward,
  building $1.75-2.50
Quaker Oats, Quaker... $3.00-5.00
Krueger Beer, Ales, waiter in
  letter "K" $1.50-2.00
Campbells Soup $4.50-6.00
Buster Brown Shoes, Buster &
  Tige $7.00-8.00

Advertising pinback buttons. First row from left: Ceresota Flour, $5.00-7.00; Black Cat Stove Polish $5.00-7.00; Otis Bed Mfg. Co. $6.00-8.00; Sharples Cream Separator Co. $6.00-8.00. Second

(Photo courtesy of Hake's Americana and Collectibles) row from left: Gold Dust Washing Powder $9.00-10.00; Wool Soap $4.00-6.00; Lacqueret $4.00-6.00; Lanes Pills $5.00-6.00; Wilburs Cocoa $6.00-8.00; Lion Coffee $4.00-6.50.

Advertising Cards

Advertising trade cards are small cards promoting products that appeared in this country in the late 19th and early 20th centuries. Usually colorful and many times comical, these little cards have become bery popular with collectors. Tobacco, alcohol, transportation and medicine cards are currently the most popular. Prices are for cards in near mint condition.

Advertising cards. National Cash Register, $8.00-10.00; Daisy Air Rifles, $2.00; Fairbanks Scales, $1.00; Howes Scales $1.50; L&M Woodhull $1.00; Columbus Buggy Co., mechanical $10.00; Hotchkiss and Company revolving cannon $5.00; Mica Axle Grease $2.50; Davis, Gould & Col $2.00; Columbus Buggy Co. $2.00; Wise's Axle Grease $1.75.

Advertising cards. White Star Soap $1.00 each; Fiske Japanese Soap **$1.00; French Laundry Soap $1.00; White Swan Soap $1.00.**

Blairs Stationery,
   schoolboy $1.00-1.50
Montgomery Ward, book
   department $1.00-1.25
Emerson Pianos, girl dancing
   with dog............ $1.50-1.75
Clark ONT Thread,
   elephant............ $1.25-1.50
Old Kentucky Tobacco . $4.00-5.00
Wilburs Cocoa $2.00-2.50
Sniders Catsup,
   mechanical $3.00-3.75

Bakers Cocoa, woman
   carrying tray $2.50-3.00
McCormick Machines, shape
   of hands............ $2.00-3.00
Kemp & Burpee, Manure
   spreader $1.50-2.00
Bradley Phosphate, Indian
   and corn $1.50-2.50
Lenox Chocolates,
   flowers............. $1.00-1.25
Pettijohn, bear $1.00-1.50
New York Weekly $4.00-5.00

Advertising cards. Teagues Inhalent $1.50; Duffy's Malt Whiskey $2.25; Kress Tonic $1.50; Schiffmann's Asthma Cure $2.25; Philip Best Brewing Co. $2.00; Hurts Remedy $1.25; Radways Ready Relief $1.75;

Heinz Pickles, girl in
  pickle $2.00-2.50
Globe Lawn Mower $1.25-1.50
Lantz Brothers Soap, baby
  on cushion $1.00-1.25
Quaker Bitters, Grover
  Cleveland $5.00-6.00
Lutteds Cough Drops, man
  in snow shoes $1.00-1.75

Uncle Sam's Nerve Liniment $2.25; Taylors Cherokee Remedy $1.75; Sanfords Ginger $4.50; Red Star Cough Cure $1.00; Hibbards Rheumatic Syrup $2.00.

Advertising Collectibles
The multimillion dollar a year advertising industry in America has provided the collector with an infinite number of trays, toys, signs, mirrors and other novelties. Anything featuring the advertiser's name is considered collectible, whether it is an ad torn from a

11

magazine or one of the many items given away as sales aids or premiums. Give-aways from the Coca-Cola Company still head the list of popular advertising collectibles followed closely by other soft drink companies. Beer advertising and cigarette advertising are also very popular. Planters' "Mr. Peanut" items are increasing rapidly in popularity. Beware of reproductions.

Sign, Mail Pouch cardboard, 20", Indians hunting fowl $25.00-30.00
Tray, Dr. Pepper, girl holding bottles $125.00-150.00
Tray, Moxie, flowers, 6" round $85.00-95.00
Tray, Modox, Shaped like Indian $125.00-150.00
Door push, Canada Dry, 11" tall, tin $15.00-20.00
Match holder, Buster Brown bread, 6" tall . . . . Rare
Match holder, Juicy Fruit, 4¾" tall, tin $50.00-60.00
Pocket Mirror, Gillette Razor, baby $35.00-50.00
Pocket Mirror, Majestic Theaters, man in glasses $25.00-30.00
Dye Cabinet, Diamond, wood, kids with balloons . . . $200.00-225.00
Spool cabinet, Clark, wood, 6-drawer . . . . $450.00 +
Dye cabinet, Putnam, wood with label $150.00-165.00
Stand-up, Fyr-Fyter, boy with extinguisher, 14" $25.00
Dispenser, Hires Root Beer, metal . . . . $200.00 +
Display case, Slidewell collars, glass and wood . . . . . . $400.00 +
Wall clock, Sauers Extracts . . . . $500.00 +
String holder, Heinz, shape of pickle, tin . . . . $500.00 +
Radio, Pepsi, bottle shape . . . . $500.00 +

The 1932 KELLOGGS Funny Jungleland can be found for about $5.00-$7.00.

Pitcher, Quaker Oats, plastic, head of Quaker $15.00-17.50
Cup, china, Ovaltine $200.00
Thermometer, Doans Pills, wood $50.00-60.00
Sign, Peter Schuylers cigar, porcelain $65.00-75.00
Mug, Chase-Sanborn Coffee, 1890's $60.00-75.00
Letter opener, Borden, Elsie the Cow, brass $10.00-12.00
Booklet, Jello, girl with tray $3.00-4.50
Clock, Calumet Baking Powder . . . . $350.00 +
Playing cards, Nu Grape Soda, 1920's $10.00-25.00
Sign, Old a keller whiskey, tin, 23 x 17 . . . . $100.00-125.00
Sign, Beech Nut Tobacco, Cardboard, Dizzy Dean $150.00-165.00
Stand up, Charles Denby Cigars 20" bellhop, 34" . $75.00-100.00

Hires Root Beer trays.

Four corner signs. Each is valued at $200.00 or more.

A group of signs. $100.00-$115.00.

Advertising Dolls

Many companies have offered dolls as premiums over the years. These dolls advertising products and services are available in a wide range of price with some early scarce dolls bringing hundreds of dollars. Many can still be found in the $10.00 and under range and some advertisers still offer dolls as premiums.

Campbell Kid doll made by Horsman in 1947, $125.00+.

Alka Seltzer, Speedy, 5½", vinyl
doll bank $7.50-9.50
Aunt Jemima, cloth, 15"
1905 . . . . $50.00-75.00
Babbit Cleanser, trademark boy,
15" composition & cloth,
1916 . . . . $175.00-200.00
Buster Brown Shoes, Buster Brown,
13" cloth, 1902 . . . . $50.00-60.00

Cal-Neva Club, Indian, 6½",
rubber, 1950's $8.00-10.00
Ceresota Flour, farmer boy,
16", cloth, 1912 . $125.00-225.00
Chesty Potato Chips, chesty
boy, 1950's $10.00-12.00

Mr. Clean from 1961 is made by Ideal and worth about $20.00.

Gerber Baby doll from 1936, cloth, rare.

Cream of Wheat, chef, cloth,
1930's $30.00-35.00

Eskimo Pie, Eskimo boy,
cloth, 1960's $6.00-7.50

Flintstone Vitamins, Fred Flintstone, inflatable $6.00-7.50

General Electric, band leader,
wood . . . . Rare

Gortons Codfish, fisherman,
7½" vinyl $8.00-10.00

Keebler, elf, 6½" vinyl,
1970's $5.00-7.50

Kelloggs, Toucan Sam, 1960's
cloth $6.00-7.50

This cloth Quisp doll is worth about $5.00-7.00

Mr. Clean, Mr. Clean doll, 1961,
vinyl, 8" $20.00-25.00

Nestle, Little Hans, 1960's,
12½" vinyl $20.00-25.00

Philip Morris, Johnny, 15", composition & cloth . . $75.00-100.00

RCA, Sellin' Fool, wood, 1920's,
15½" $150.00-200.00

Seven Up, Fresh-up Freddie, 1950's,
cloth & rubber, 24" $25.00-30.00

Sunshine Animal Crackers, Elephant, 5½", cloth . $40.00-50.00

Akro Agate

Akro Agate was a producer of Depression glass and marbles that specialized in children's dishes. Some pieces are opaque and have a "marbleized" look to them. Entire sets of children's dishes in the original boxes are premium items, especially Play Time and American Maid tea sets. Some pieces are marked with a crow flying through the letter A, carrying a marble in its beak and each claw.

Children's dishes

Creamer, concentric ring
pattern $2.00-5.00

Saucer, Raised Daisy . . . $6.00-7.50

Sugar with lid, Raised
Daisy $20.00-22.00

Cup, Akro Luster, jade . $4.50-6.00

Plate, Akro Duster, pink $3.50-4.00

Pitcher, octagonal,
open handle $9.00-11.50

Cup, octagonal, closed
handle $7.00-8.00

Sugar, no lid, octagonal,
closed handle $10.00-12.00

Creamer, Stacked Disc,
white $2.00-3.00

Teapot with lid,
Stacked Disc $4.00-4.75

Saucer, Interior Panel . . $2.75-3.50

Plate, Interior Panel . . . $3.25-4.50

Creamer, marbleized . . $8.00-12.00

Sugar, marbleized $7.00-8.50

Miscellaneous

Lamp, marbleized,
wall type $35.00-45.00

Jardiniere, 5" $6.00-7.00

Lamp, marbleized . . . $40.00-50.00

Flower pot, 4",
marbleized $4.00-5.00

Candlesticks, pair, 3¼",
marbleized $12.00-15.00

Two boxed sets of Akro Agate children's dishes in original boxes showing the distinct shape of the glassware, $200.00-300.00.

Armand Marseille Dolls

These dolls were manufactured in Germany in the late 1800's and early 1900's by the family of Armand Marseille. The dolls have painted porcelain heads at one time were being produced in greater numbers than any of the other dolls from Europe. Most dolls are marked with an "A.M.". Some are marked "Made in Germany" or "Germany". Don't confuse these with dolls produced in the late 1800's and early 1900's by M.J. Moehling that were also marked with an "AM".

12" Baby Phyllis . . . . $225.00 +
12" Darling Baby . . $145.00-160.00
12" Duchess $100.00-125.00
7" Socket head, Just Me $400.00 +
9" Kiddiejoy, open mouth,
   1918 . . . . $150.00-170.00

18" Rosebud, 1902 . . . . . $225.00 +
7½" all bisque,
   socket head $125.00-150.00
16" Bumble Puppy, 1909 $225.00 +
7" rubber body, Wee One,
   black, 1922 . . . . . $180.00-200.00
12" Baby Love, 1914,
   socket head . . . . $200.00 +
9" Oriental, socket head $285.00 +
18" Our Ann, 1900 $185.00-200.00
15" Gold Coast Girl,
   1905 . . . . $100.00-125.00
29" shoulder head, My Princess,
   1905 . . . . $225.00 +
21" shoulder head, Miss Myrtle,
   1899 . . . . $250.00 +
17½" shoulder head, Little
   Sweetheart, 1902 $150.00-175.00
16½" socket head,
   My Dearie . . . . $350.00 +
18" socket head, Patrice $225.00 +
11½" socket head, Gibson
   Girl . . . . $500.00 +

11" socket head, Louisa,
  1915 . . . . $75.00-100.00
8" infant, Berry . . . . . . $250.00 +
26" socket head, Dorothy,
  1912 . . . . $350.00 +
20" open/closed mouth, Hoopla
  Girl, 1916 . . . . $400.00 +
22" shouler head, painted eyes,
  Bernadet, 1909 . . . . . . $300.00 +

24" socket head, closed mouth,
  Beatrice, 1912 . . . . . . $300.00 +
10" Mimi, 1922 . . . $115.00-130.00
10" Possy, 1910 . . . $145.00-160.00
20" Clara, 1928 . . . . $300.00 +
24" socket head, Wonderful
  Alice . . . . $200.00 +
7½" open/closed mouth,
  Jutta, 1908 . . . . . $150.00-175.00

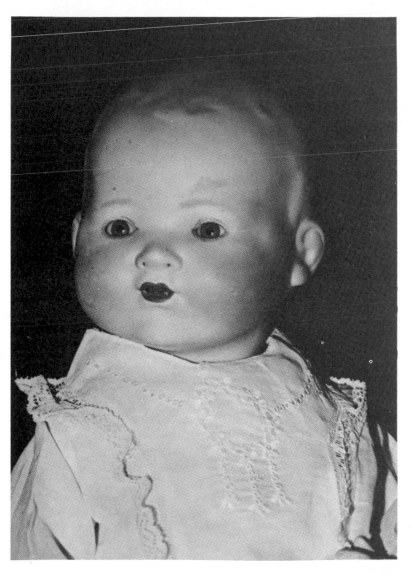

This Armand Marseille 16" doll, My Baby, is worth about $200.00.

12'' shoulder head doll, $65.00.

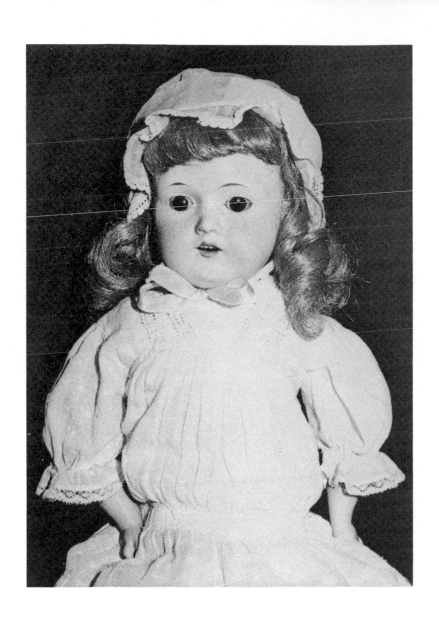

12'' socket head doll, $65.00.

Art Deco

Art Deco first appeared at the Paris Exhibition in the mid 1920's and continued in popularity into the 1940's. The designs of Art Deco are generally angular with simplicity of line and movement emphasized. Sensuous nudes, Egyptian characters and bold geometric designs, graphics, and other products of the period. Don't confuse this with Art Nouveau, an earlier art form that also used sensuous flowing nude figures.

Lamp, nude and dog on
 base $55.00-65.00
Bookends, nude and two
 Wolfhounds $30.00-40.00
Bracelet, silver & enamel,
 Egyptian motif ...... $100.00 +
Clock, electric, onyx and
 marble .... $100.00 +
Tray, Tiffany, silver,
 handled .... $500.00 +
Ashtray, iron, Scottie
 dog $10.00-12.00
Bookends, copper plate,
 nudes $30.00-35.00

Candleholder, ceramic, bold
 geometric design $8.00-12.00
Lamp, nude stepping over glass
 ball, bronze finish . $50.00-75.00
Figurine, Flapper girl dancing,
 bronze $175.00-200.00
Bookends, chrome, dancing
 nudes $10.00-15.00
Ashtray, nude girl holding bowl,
 bronze $25.00-35.00
Smokers stand, partially nude
 woman holding ashtray,
 30" $150.00-175.00
Powder box, chrome & enamel,
 mirror $40.00-45.00

Cigarette case, gold plate &
 silver plate,
 woman's head $50.00-75.00
Magazine holder, leaping dog,
 cast iron $50.00-60.00
Wall match holder,
 flapper $12.00-15.00
Salt shaker, fish, round glass
 with silver base $35.00-50.00
Figurine, tiger,
 bronze $100.00-125.00
Candlesticks, chrome,
 round $30.00-40.00

Bookends from the Art Deco period. The partially nude girl and Egyptian influence are key ingredients to Art Deco. The pair would sell for $30.00-$40.00.

Necklace, chrome & bakelite,
  multicolor $25.00-35.00
Pin, silver, amethyst,
  enameled birds with
  large wings $100.00-125.00
Steamship brochure, blue &
  silver cover, "Ile de
  France" $25.00-35.00

Lamp, back to back bronze
  nudes supporting 5 tiered
  shade .... $200.00 +
Perfume bottle, glass,
  bird stopper $60.00-75.00

This Art Deco ashtray that incor-
porates a female figure as its base
has a bronze finish and is worth
about $25.00.

Art Nouveau

Art nouveau, or new art, became
popular in the 1890's and continued
until around the first World War. It
is noted for its themes of nature,
especially flowers and the sea, and
use of sensuous nudes in graceful
flowing lines. Like Art Deco, it
entered all facets of art and life and
can be seen in glassware, furniture,
architecture, jewelry, graphics, etc.
Art Nouveau is a forerunner of Art
Deco and the influence can be seen
easily. L. Tiffany is probably the
most noted producer of Art
Nouveau work, with signed pieces
bringing thousands of dollars.
Beware of reproductions in Art
Nouveau collecting.

An electric Art Deco style lamp,
$50.00-75.00.

Planter, ducks on base,
  chrome $25.00-35.00
Mug, cobalt blue in
  silver holder $25.00-35.00
Earrings, enamel, multicolor
  geometric design ... $12.00-17.00
Dressing screen, castle against
  moon in center .. $150.00-200.00

Clothing brush, silverplate,
long-haired girl and
flowers $20.00-25.00
Tie clip, gold, girl's head $125.00 +
Mirror & brush, girls with flowing
hair, silverplate $60.00-70.00
Inkwell, bronze base with four
heads, glass well . . $75.00-100.00
Pin tray, nude and cupid,
silver . . . . $100.00 +
Buckle, nude, brass . . $15.00-20.00
Hairbrush, nude handle, flowers
and cupids, silver . . . . $100.00 +
Watch fob, woman's head,
brass $8.00-12.00

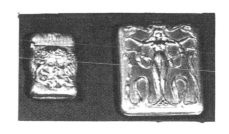

**Art Nouveau match safe and
cigarette holder. Silver with gold
wash from about 1910. Each is
worth $150.00-200.00.**

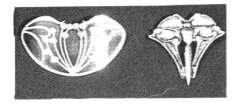

**Two Art Nouveau brooches. The
one at left is copper and silver and is
valued at $65.00. The brooch on the
right is silver with mother of pearl
inlay, $65.00.**

Locket, silver, floral
design $60.00-75.00
Ashtray, bronze, nude holding
bowl on knee $50.00-65.00
Clock, iron and brass, angels
and gargoyles $65.00-75.00
Bookmark, silver, heart shape
with woman $40.00-55.00
Candlestick, pewter,
iris $30.00-45.00
Bookends, bronze, nude and
pool $65.00-85.00
Picture frame, silver, nude figure
and flowers $50.00-75.00
Pin, snake, sterling silver $150.00 +
Belt buckle, double iris,
silver $70.00-80.00
Picture frame, floral decor,
metal $25.00-30.00

Candle holders, brass, triple leaves
make base $40.00-50.00
Soap dish, sterling, cherub and
woman $100.00-115.00
Dresser set, mirror, 3 brushes,
jar, silver, raised
flowers $135.00-150.00
Match holder, bisque, woman
and swan $25.00-30.00
Decanter, ceramic, nude
handle . . . . $200.00 +
Belt buckle, lizards and flowers,
silverplate $30.00-35.00
Letter holder, brass, female
figures $50.00-60.00
Fireplace cover, tin and copper
with cherubs $150.00-165.00
Letter seal, silver with initial
and flower handle . . $20.00-25.00
Paper clip, bronze, girls head
on clover $15.00-20.00

Art Pottery

Art pottery first appeared in the
United States around 1870. After
that time many companies began to
produce art pottery. Some of the
most popular producers were
Roseville, Rookwood, Van Brigle
and Weller. The collector should
take the utmost caution in this field
to avoid reproductions. Pieces signed by the artist are the best but
many pieces are unsigned and unmarked.

Peters & Reed, vase,
  Aztec Moss $35.00-50.00
Rookwood, vase, blue flowers,
  artist signed $175.00-200.00
Rookwood, vase, elk,
  artist signed .... $500.00 +
Van Briggle, bowl, frogs &
  dragonfly....... $125.00-150.00

Zanesville, vase, clover,
  artist signed $175.00-200.00
Zanesville, vase,
  wild rose $75.00-100.00
Rookwood vase,
  fish $125.00-150.00
Norse, Iron age vase
  copy $25.00-40.00

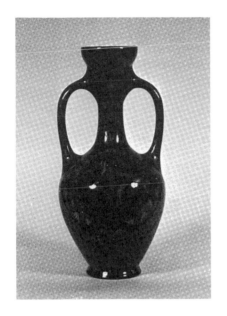

Gouda art pottery. This type of pottery from Holland is very popular and each of these vases is worth around $200.00.

Four pieces of Rookwood pottery, about $200.00 or more.
all artist signed. Each is valued at

Boch art pottery

Autographs

Autographs and autographed documents and photos of the famous are treasures to some collectors. Many types of personalities are considered collectible, whether it be sports figures, presidents, historical figures or motion picture stars. Values fluctuate greatly and rapidly in this category, especially in items considered to be rare. Age is not the only consideration when evaluating an autograph. The importance of the individual, the type of document involved and the number of the individual's autographs available have much influence on the market value. The prices here should be used as a comparative guide. Be especially careful to avoid forgeries and misrepresentations in this area. Old stock certificates and other documents are good sources for autographs.

F. Scott Fitzgerald, card signed,
1920's $175.00-185.00
James Thurber, letter,
1960's $50.00-65.00
Howard Hughes, signed
photograph $225.00
Dr. Martin Luther King Jr.,
signed photograph . $35.00-45.00
Louis Armstrong, signed
program $25.00-30.00
Mel Blanc, signature . $10.00-15.00
Marilyn Monroe, signed
letter $135.00-150.00
Samuel F.B. Morse, letter,
1860's . . . . $900.00 +
Frank James, signed letter,
1880's . . . . $700.00 +

A. Lincoln

Abraham Lincoln signed many letters and documents in his lifetime, as a lawyer, statesman, and president. Lincoln material is valuable but beware of the many imitations on the market.

Larry Fine (Three Stooges),
signature $30.00-32.50
Warren G. Harding, signed document, 1919 . . . . . . $115.00-125.00
Franklin Roosevelt, signed
White House Card . $27.50-32.00
John Quincy Adams, letter,
1840's . . . . $1000.00 +
Robert E. Lee, letter while general,
1860's . . . . $400.00 +
Abraham Lincoln, document signed
as lawyer . . . . $1750 +
Rudyard Kipling, letter,
1930's $225.00-250.00
John D. Rockefeller, letter,
1915 . . . . $100.00-125.00
Jefferson Davis, letter while
Secretary of War $125.00-150.00
James Garfield, letter,
1880 . . . . $125.00-150.00
William T. Sherman, letter,
late 1800's $125.00-135.00
Thomas Dewey,
signature $10.00-12.00
Ulysses Grant, letter signed
while president . . $175.00-225.00
Theodore Roosevelt,
signature $35.00-50.00
Jack Dempsey,
signature $10.00-12.00
Pat Garret, signed warrant,
1880's $275.00-300.00

Thos A Edison

The signature of Thomas Edison, inventor and entrepreneur, can be found on stock certificates from several companies. A stock certificate with Edison's signature is valued at about $500.00.

28

Automobile Collectibles

Since the price of antique automobiles is very restrictive to most collectors, many have turned to collecting materials dealing with automobiles. Actual accessories as well as owners manuals, shop manuals, advertisements, catalogs and posters featuring the cars of yesterday have become very collectible. Anything made through the 1950's is considered collectible and even some later items. But, generally, the more valuable items are from the 1930's or before. Be on the lookout for items from or about automobiles or their producing companies that are no longer in existence.

Owners manual, Ford Model A,
    1928 . . . . $12.00-15.00
Catalog, Plymouth,
    1939 . . . . $17.50-20.00
Tire pump, brass,
    Ford $20.00-30.00
Shop manual, De Soto,
    1950's $7.50-10.00
Radiator emblem,
    Franklin $20.00-22.50
Dash clock, New Haven $50.00
Radiator cap, Pontiac,
    Indian $25.00-35.00
Spark plug wrench,
    Ford $7.50-10.00

This 1953 Plymouth catalog is valued at $3.50-5.00.

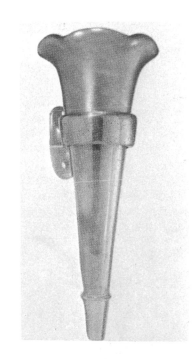

This carnival glass car vase is possibly from a Packard and worth about $15.00-20.00.

Hood ornament, brass, Mercury,
    1920's $35.00-45.00
Headlamps, Model T,
    pair $100.00
Parts list, Cadillac,
    1916 . . . . $8.00-12.00
Parts catalog, Essex,
    1920's $7.50-10.00
Hood ornament, bulldog,
    Mack $25.00-35.00
Advertising postcard, 1940 Dodge
    1½ ton truck $3.00-5.00
Postcard, 1936 Pontiac
    "8" $2.00-4.00

Aviation Collectibles

Anything dealing with airplanes and flight, either civilian or military is highly collectible. Items concerning zeppelins or lighter-than-air craft are especially popular among aviation collectors. Lindberg and related materials are also popular items,

Charles A. Lindbergh (autograph)

Autograph of Charles Lindberg $100.00.

and there is a multitude of collectibles available in this area.

Photo postcard, American Airlines, 1930's, plane $3.00-6.00

Photo postcard, American Airlines, 1930's, stewardess . . . $5.00-7.50

Magazine, *Aerial Age Weekly*, 1920's $3.00-5.00

Pilot's helmet, leather, 1920's $25.00-35.00

Flight schedule, American Airlines, 1930's $12.00-15.00

Baggage label, zeppelin, round, paper $15.00-25.00

Book, *Wings* 1920's . . $10.00-12.00

Autographed letter, Amelia Erhart, 1930's $250.00

Autographed letter, Orville Wright, 1930's $175.00

Window sticker "Buy a bomber, Slap a Jap", 1940's . . $1.00-2.00

Propeller, wood & metal, 8 ft. long $200.00

Army flight manual, World War I $15.00-20.00

Postcard, Charles Lindberg & plane $7.50-8.00

Booklet, "Know Your War Planes", Coca-Cola, 1943 . . . . $20.00-30.00

Cards, Fighting Planes, Coca-Cola, set of 20, 1943 . . . . . $35.00-45.00

Pinback, Wright Bros. Celebration, 1909 . . . . $12.00-15.00

Pinback, Eastern Airlines, New York to Wash. 80 Minute Man $5.00-6.50

These pilot badges are from the caps of World War II Luftwaffe pilots. **The cloth officers badge is worth $100.00. The enlisted badge, $35.00.**

Avon

Avon began as the California Perfume Company in the 1880's and has grown to become one of the largest perfume manufacturers and distributors in the world. Collectors across the country consider these products collectible and many, especially early products, are quite valuable to the serious collector. Perfume bottles are popular and so are food coloring kits, soaps, nearly any figural container and many other Avon products. Prices haven't increased much on area in the last year or so.

Avon Perfection food coloring set,
  1935, complete ... $75.00-100.00
Silver Cream polish,
  1920's............ $30.00-45.00

An Avon 1968 Scimitar after shave lotion bottle, 10'', $10.00-$15.00.

Powdered Cleaner,
  1933 .... $20.00-25.00
Beauty Basket, 1947 .. $75.00-80.00
Color Magic Set,
  1940's............ $30.00-40.00
Vanity set in box,
  1930's............ $50.00-55.00
Lucy Hays Perfume,
  1936 .... $50.00-60.00
Daisy Shampoo, 1950's . $7.50-8.50
Sea Horse, 1971 ...... $7.50-10.00
Classic Decanter, 1970 .. $5.00-7.50
Whale Organizer,
  1973 .... $25.00-30.00

Black Sheep set, 1955 . $50.00-60.00
Bay Rum soap, 1954 . $20.00-25.00
Hidden Treasure Soap,
  1974 .... $4.00-6.00

Avon car bottles from 1968 and 1969 worth about $3.00-7.00 each.

Spongaroo Soap and Sponge,
  1966 .... $10.00-12.00
Santa's Helper Soap,
  1955 .... $50.00-60.00
Avonlite Soap on a Rope,
  bowling ball, 1961 . $30.00-40.00
Toofie Tooth Paste,
  1967 .... $4.00-6.50
Rolls Royce, 1972 ...... $7.00-8.00
Furniture polish, 1916 $60.00-70.00
Cleansing Cream Demo Kit,
  1947 .... $27.00-32.00
Inkwell, 1970 .... $5.00-7.00
Super Shaver, 1973 ..... $2.50-5.00
Alpine Flask, 1966 ... $40.00-50.00

Badges

Collectors have gradually picked up law enforcement badges until they are now considered to be popular items. Once only popular with collectors of old west memorabilia, badges are now collectible on their own merit. Most collectible of the badges are those in gold or silver, but nickel, brass or combinations are also very popular. Unusual badges, express badges, and old badges from famous western towns are much sought after by collectors. The collector should be careful to purchase only authentic badges because there are some reproductions on the market.

City Marshall, 6 point star,
early $85.00-125.00
Dallas Police, eagle and shield,
plain, early $225.00-275.00
Galveston Police, shield, plain,
early $275.00-350.00
Butte Police, star and shield, 1900,
nickel over brass . $175.00-225.00
City Police, star in circle, hard
engraved, early . . $175.00-225.00
Deputy Sheriff, star and crescent,
1890, gold . . . . Rare
Chief of Police, seven point star,
sterling silver, 1900's . $350.00 +
Police, octagon, nickel plated brass.
1900 . . . . $35.00-65.00
Deputy Marshal, United States, I.T.
(Indian Territory) star and crescent, nickel silver . . . . Rare
Deputy Sheriff, Custer Co.
Montana, shield and eagle,
early $175.00-225.00
City Police, shield, nickel silver
engraved, early
1900's $135.00-165.00
Denver Police, five point star,
nickel silver, early . . . . $450.00 +
American Express Co., Special
Agent, shield and star . $350.00 +

This nickel silver badge from Lander Wyoming is from the early 1900's and worth about $150.00 or more.

American Railway Express Co.,
Special Officer, circle and
star $150.00-200.00
City Marshal, six point star,
silver, 1900 . . . . . $150.00-200.00

Banks, Mechanical

Mechanical banks are iron, brightly colored banks that perform some kind of action when a coin is placed in the bank. There are between 235 and 250 known types of mechanical banks produced between the Civil War and World War I. Be very cautious because many reproductions have been produced. Though most of these reproductions can be distinguished from the old banks, many are made to appear as the originals.

William Tell . . . . $225.00 +
Professor Pug Frog's Great
Bicycle Feat . . . . $450.00 +
Football . . . . $400.00 +
Butting Buffalo . . . . $400.00 +
Dog & Turn Table $175.00
Chief Big Moon . . . . $400.00 +

Man riding Elephant $150.00
Mason Bank . . . . $400.00 +
Indian & Bear . . . . $200.00 +
Punch & Judy . . . . $200.00 +
Atlas Bank . . . . $250.00 +
Hoop-La . . . . $250.00 +
Magician . . . . $275.00 +
Stump Speaker . . . . $250.00 +
Artillery Bank . . . . $200.00 +
Lion Hunter . . . . $450.00 +
Dancing Bear . . . . $500.00 +
World's Fair . . . . $275.00 +
Chinaman . . . . $275.00 +
Squirrel . . . . $325.00 +
Grenadier . . . . $200.00 +
Organ Grinder & Monkey . $200.00
Acrobat . . . . $225.00 +
Mother & Baby Eagles . . $200.00 +
Uncle Sam . . . . $200.00 +
Lion & Monkeys . . . . $200.00 +
Darktown Battery . . . . . . $250.00 +
Trick Pony . . . . $200.00 +
Trick Dog . . . . $200.00 +

**Humpty Dumpty mechanical bank.
Put a coin in the clown's hand and
he pops it into his mouth. This bank
is valued at about $200.00.**

**This mechanical bank is known as
"Teddy and the Bear". When a coin
is placed on the gun barrel and the**
switch thrown, the coin is shot into
the tree and a bear pops out the top.
An original is worth over $350.00.

Banks Still

Still banks are generally constructed of tin, cast iron, aluminum, pot metal, or glass and have no working parts with the exception of wheels. They were produced in a variety of styles and types, from characters to buildings, cars and animals. Following the war years, military vehicles and heroes were very popular. Some banks were used as advertisement and given away as premiums. Value depends on rarity, quality and type, as well as condition.

T. Roosevelt, bust, iron,
5" $50.00-60.00
Billiken Shoes,
Elfax 4¼ ". $35.00-45.00
Lindberg bust,
aluminum $50.00-60.00
Daffy Duck with tree,
pot metal $15.00-20.00
Mickey Mouse,
aluminum $75.00-100.00
Rabbit, cast iron, 6" . $45.00-50.00
Elephant, Jumbo Savings Bank,
tin $15.00-20.00

Goose, Red Goose Shoes,
iron $35.00-45.00
Bear, stealing pig, iron .. $125.00 +

This cast iron bull dog is worth about $50.00.

Brinks Armored Truck,
die cast $35.00-40.00
Graf Zeppelin $50.00-75.00

Bugs Bunny leaning on a tree and standing by a barrel. These pot metal banks are worth about $25.00-35.00 each.

Airplane, tin, 8" $45.00-55.00
Battleship Maine $85.00-95.00
German Ship, lead, 7" $35.00-45.00
Woolworth Building,
　8" $65.00-75.00
Castle, 4" $40.00-50.00
Independence Hall, glass,
　7" $75.00-100.00
Eiffle Tower, 8" $75.00-85.00
Statue of Liberty, 6" . $45.00-55.00
Kodak Bank $45.00-55.00
Lion on wheels, 5" ... $75.00-80.00
Horse, prancing, 4" .. $25.00-35.00
Tank, World War II,
　iron $60.00-80.00
Taxi, iron, 2½" $85.00-100.00
Elephant, cast iron,
　4" $30.00-40.00
Squirrel, iron, 4" $30.00-40.00
Trolley car, 3" $65.00-75.00
Fort Dearborn, 6" ... $35.00-50.00
Dog & Windmill, tin
　3½" $20.00-30.00
Shell bank, 8" $25.00-30.00
Top hat, 2¼" $20.00-25.00
Owl on stump, 5" $50.00-65.00
Deer, 9" $30.00-40.00
Panda bear, die cast,
　4½" $30.00-40.00
Horse, on wheels $65.00-80.00
Washington Monument,
　7½" $45.00-55.00

Barbed Wire

Barbed wire was the result of more than one man's idea on armored fencing but Joseph Glidden is usually credited with the invention. Within ten years of the date of his patent in 1874, the plains was crossed with barbed wire fences. The need to protect crops from cattle and buffalo on the plains and later to enclose the cattle was the basis for barbed wire. The lack of wood on the plains made it necessary to locate another source of inexpensive fencing material. Prices here are for 18" strands.

Single round line, 2 point barb

Baker's single strand,
　1894 .... $2.00-3.50
Levi M. Devore, 1875 .... Rare
Micheal Kelly, 1885 .... Rare
Sunderland kink, 1884 ... $.50-1.25
Sunderland, no kink,
　1884 .... $.50-1.25

Double round line, 2 point barb

Bakers flat barb,
　1882 .... $1.00-2.00
Decker Spread, 1884 ... $1.00-1.50
Glidden long barb
　(hog wire) $1.00-2.00
Rose's modern .... $.50-.75
Salisbury 1876 ...... $35.00-40.00

A barbed wire patented by C. Kennedy in 1875. An eighteen inch strand is valued at $6.00-8.00. An 1881 patented barbed wire called Gunderson two point is worth about $3.00-5.00.

Single round line, 4 point barb

Booth, 1875 .... Rare
Hill, 1876 .... $2.50-5.00
Merrills skeleton,
　1876 .... $4.00-6.00
Allen, 1875 .... $15.00-17.50
Saddle barb, 1876 ...... $1.25-3.75

Double round line, 4 point barb

Lenox, 1883 . . . . Rare
Stevens, 1879 . . . . $10.00-12.00
Upham, 1881 . . . . $4.50-7.00
Wing's V Barb, 1878 . . . $3.00-5.00
Randall, 1877 . . . . $3.50-5.00

Single round line, plate barb

Armstrong, 1876 . . . . Rare
George Baker $50.00-75.00
Supr Barb, 1881 . . . . $150.00 +
Stover Barb, 1875 . . . . $15.00-20.00
Washer Barb, 1878 . . . $10.00-15.00

Barber Collectibles

Barber and grooming collectibles include items for home use as well as those used solely in barbershops.

Shaving mugs were popular in the latter part of the 19th century and demand high prices when found in good condition. Barbershop furnishings and barber tools are also picking up a large following.

Shaving stand with mirror, oak, 1900 . . . . $350.00
Barber chair, porcelain and iron, leather seat & back $200.00
Barber chair - oak and brass, leather seat and back $1,000.00 +
Shaving mug rack, oak with pigeonholes, carved top . $300.00
Advertising pocket mirror, Gillet Safety Razor $15.00-17.50
Bottle, paneled opaline "Witch Hazel" in gold script $60.00-70.00

A selection of barber collectibles: wood-handled curlers, wood-handled brush, razor blade in package and tin saver, hand clippers and straight razor.

Hand clippers, metal,
1920's $10.00-20.00
Bottle, porcelain, handpainted
roses, "Bay Rum" . $60.00-70.00
Photo, tin type, barber in shop,
late 1800's $20.00-40.00
Shaving mug, blacksmith shoeing
horse, late 1800's $125.00-135.00
Shaving mug, dentist, late
1800's $150.00-160.00
Shaving mug, mail wagon and horse,
late 1800's $125.00-135.00
Shaving mug, streetcar, late
1800's $110.00-120.00
Shaving mug, carnation, late
1800's $15.00-17.50
Razor strap, leather, Double
Duck $10.00-12.00
Shoeshine stand, wood base,
wrought iron chair &
footrest $200.00-300.00
Shoeshine chair, oak on wood base
with iron footrest $500.00
Barber pole, wood, red, white &
blue, 5' high $100.00

Barbie Dolls & Collectibles

In the past 18 years nearly 100
million Barbie dolls have been sold.
Most Barbie dolls on the market today can be bought for around $5.00.
But many of the accessories
however, bring much higher prices.
There are many collectors of Barbie
dolls and related materials today
and the values of some of the more
rare items are increasing. The values
here are for used items but still in
excellent condition.

The original Barbie Doll from 1959.
This dolls has pointed eyebrows,
white irises, and a different type of
hair than the more modern version.
One of these dolls would be worth
about $50.00.

Barbie's Airplane $18.00-25.00
Barbies ballerina stage . $7.00-10.00
Barbie's boat, (Sears) . . $7.00-10.00
Barbie's Classy
Corvette $10.00-12.00
Barbie colorforms $2.00-3.50
Barbie's Fashion Shop $12.00-15.00
Queen of the Prom game $2.00-4.50
Olympic gym $3.00-5.00

Swimming pool $3.50-6.00
Skipper's Dream
Room $10.00-15.00
Ski Village $5.00-7.00
Ballerina Barbie $3.00-5.00
Free Moving Barbie $3.00-5.00
Malibu Barbie $2.00-4.00
Free Moving Ken $3.00-5.00
Gold Medal Skier Ken . . $3.00-5.00

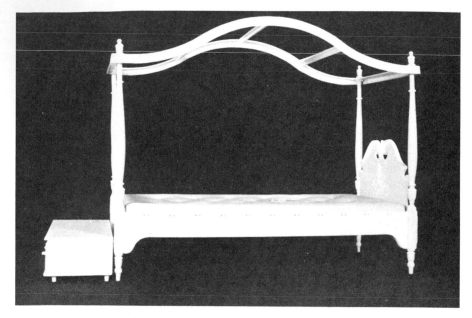

This Barbie's fourposter bed and chest from the early 1960's is worth about $5.00-10.00.

Baseball Cards

Baseball cards were first issued in the United States before the turn of the Century. They were small, around 1½'' x 2½'', generally of poor quality and given away with tobacco and cigarettes. In the 1930's chewing gum companies began to produce baseball cards and have continued to date, most popular card producers being Bowman and Topps. The most treasured cards are

From the Bowman 1952 issue, Leo Durocher, $3.00-5.00, and Pete Suder, $1.00. The Enos Slaughter is worth $3.00-5.00 and is a 1954 Bowman.

Phil Rizzuto and Billy Martin, Card #93, Bowman 1953 is worth about $2.00. The card measures 2½ x 3¾.

the color, photo cards of the 1930's. Any baseball great or Hall of Famer is generally more valuable than the other players in a particular issue year.

Bowman, 1950, color, . . $2.00-2.50
Bowman, 1951, color . . . $1.50-2.00
Bowman, 1955 . . . . $.50-1.00

Topps, 1951, players on
   diamond . . . . $.75-1.50
Topps, 1953, color . . . . . . $.75-1.50
Topps, 1954 color $1.00-1.25
Topps, 1955, team inset
   & autograph . . . . $.50-1.00
Topps, 1956 similar to
   1955 . . . . $.25-1.25
Topps, 1957 color . . . . $.25-.50
Topps, 1958-1959 . . . . $.25-.50
Topps, 1960-64 . . . . $.15-.35
Topps, 1965-67 . . . . $.10-.25
Topps, 1968-Present . . . . . $.05-.10

Baseball Collectibles

The memorabilia of America's national pastime has come into the limelight as popular collectibles. The ticket stubs, player autographs, programs, scorecards, fan magazines, yearbooks, match books, photographs, postcards, uniforms, pins and trading cards of baseball have become very collectible, with values increasing. Teams no longer in existence are good to look for and so are mementoes of the more popular players and Hall of Famers.

A photo postcard from the early 1900's showing an early baseball game. $2.00-3.00.

1942 World Series Program. $12.00-15.00.

Ticket, Ebbets Field night game,
1950's $7.00-10.00

World Series Ticket, 1958,
Milwaukee Braves . $10.00-12.00

Stan Musial, plastic, Hartland
Statue, 1960's $50.00-100.00

Scorecard, St. Louis Cardinals,
1963 . . . . $2.50-3.50

Program, 1949, Chicago
Cubs $3.50-5.00

World Series Program, 1935,
Cubs and Tigers . . . $15.00-20.00

Autographed Baseball, 1951
Yankees $125.00

Matchbook, Carl Hubbell,
1930's $2.00-3.00

Yearbook, New York Yankees,
1950's $12.00-15.00

Autographed Baseball, Brooklyn
Dodgers, 1933 . . . $125.00-140.00

Yearbook, Chicago White Sox,
1959 . . . . $7.00-9.00

Pen, Baseball bat, Coca-Cola,
1940's $45.00-55.00

Hall of Fame Records, baseball
shape, Coca-Cola,
1960 . . . . $30.00-35.00

Pinback, Babe Ruth, Esso Boys
Club, 1920's $4.00-7.50

Baskets
Appreciation of basketry in the past decade has led to an increased interest in collecting baskets. Old handmade baskets are the most popular with Shaker examples at a premium. Watch out for reproductions made to appear old.

Wall basket, poplar splint,
6" tall $70.00-80.00

Herb drying basket, hex woven,
1800's . . . . $250.00 +

Half basket, ash,
hickory handle . . $150.00-175.00

Three handled basket, poplar
splint, 13" tall $75.00-85.00

Utility basket, ash, carved
oak handles $75.00-85.00

Oval field basket,
11" tall $125.00-150.00

Market basket from the early 1900's. This basket with copper riveted handles is worth $150.00 or more.

Field basket, rib type,
16'' tall, 1850's ...... $250.00 +
Field basket, splint, wood handles,
1800's.......... $175.00-200.00
Field basket, rib type,
wrap handle, 13'' tall . $250.00 +

This large field basket from the 1800's could bring as much as $200.00 or more.

Swing basket, rib type,
demijohn bottom .... $200.00 +

Nantucket light ship basket,
1900's rattan .... $350.00 +
Buttocks basket, covered,
twist handle .... $200.00 +
Shaker market basket,
1800's.......... $100.00-125.00
Gathering basket, ash, double
hickory handle, 1800's $300.00 +

Picnic basket, 1930's . $10.00-17.50

Fruit basket, ash & oak splint,
1800's........... $50.00-75.00

Beer Cans

Beer can collecting is an especially popular hobby today, particularly among younger collectors. It is a reasonably inexpensive hobby to begin but some of the early or more rare cans can bring prices of up to $100.00 or more. Most beer cans are colorful with unique designs and lend themselves well to display. The most popular cans are the cone top cans that were the earliest beer cans.

Field basket $125.00.

A group of 12 oz. cone top beer cans. Each of these cans is worth $25.00 to $50.00 with the exception of the Diehl Five Star and Cooks Gold Blume, that would bring as much as $75.00 or more.

These 12 oz. cone top beer cans are worth about $30.00-$60.00 except for Namar and Old Vienna Type, $90.00.

Beer Collectibles

With the increased interest in beer cans, there has been an increasing concern over beer advertising and related materials. Trays, signs, taps, kegs, and so forth, have become popular with values steadily rising. The color and quality of the beer items, in addition to their relative abundance have contributed strongly to this popularity. Currently beer advertising items remain high among the list of most sought after advertising collectibles.

Mug, pottery, Leisy's Light
   Beer $20.00-25.00
Mug, Independent Brewing
   Association,
   Chicago $50.00-60.00
Opera cards, Tony Faust
   Beer $5.00-7.50
Match safe, A. Busch,
   1880's $50.00-60.00
Fan, Schlitz,
   battleship $30.00-35.00

Trays

Iroquois Beer, 1905 $125.00-140.00
Jax Beer, cowboy $50.00-60.00

A pair of Schlitz tin signs from the 1890's, $250.00 for the pair.

Miller Highlife, girl on
   moon $70.00-85.00
National Brewing Co.,
   cowboys $160.00-185.00
Pabst, Brewery, 1910 ... $250.00+
Pacific Beer,
   mountain $75.00-90.00
Pabst Blue Ribbon, man pouring
   beer $40.00-50.00
Magnus Beck, brewery .. $200.00+
Dixie Beer, waitress,
   1930's $40.00-60.00

This Cataract Consumers Brewery tray from 1910 is worth about $80.00-90.00, and the Cold Springs

Brewing Co. tray from 1905 will bring from $40.00 to $50.00.

A beautiful example of beer adver- **tising. Rare.**

Signs

Golden Jubilee, baby & puppies
   tin . . . . $300.00 +
Edelweiss, girl on swing, tin with
   chain . . . . $600.00 +

Eckhart Brothers, glass,
   eagle . . . . $300.00 +
Waukesha Brewing Co.,
   cardboard . . . . $450.00 +
Blatz private stock,
   glass $75.00-100.00

Bells

Bells are made of many different materials and serve many different purposes. Though some bells were made entirely for decoration, most were created to inform the hearer of some event. There are bells to announce tea, bells to announce dinner, bells to announce the beginning of school and church and many more. Several types of metal have been used in making bells. Brass bells are especially popular.

This 6" school bell is brass with a wood handle. It will bring $30.00-40.00.

Cowbell, primitive with wooden
   clapper $30.00-40.00
Cowbell, star and crescent
   embossed $25.00-35.00
Shop bell, iron on spring
   1800's $40.00-50.00
Cowbell, brass $35.00-40.00
Ship's bell, marked "U.S.N.",
   1890's . . . . $200.00+

Sleigh bells, brass,
   set of 16 . . . . $125.00+
School bell, 11" tall, brass and
   wood $70.00-80.00
Team bell, copper $10.00-15.00
Sheep bell, copper $7.50-10.00
Turkey bell, nickel plate $4.00-6.00
Tea bell, silver plate . . $25.00-30.00
Fire bell . . . . $100.00+
School/Church bell, iron,
   mounted . . . . $150.00+
Tea bell, metal with wood
   handle $5.00-10.00
Farm bell, iron mounted on
   brackets . . . . $100.00+
Desk bell, cast iron $7.00-10.00
Train bell, brass and cast iron
   mount . . . . $300.00+
Trolley bell, iron $45.00-60.00

Big Little Books

Big Little Books first appeared in the early 1930's. They are small, (4"x4") thick books that are generally illustrated with comic strips or movie stills and were produced under several different brand names. The most desirable of the little books are those from the "Golden Age" that lasted from the late 1930's until the late 1940's. Well known comic characters are very popular with collectors and usually bring good prices. Similar books are being produced today, so the collector of "Big Little Books" should be very cautious. All prices reflect books in good to very good condition produced before 1950.

Alley Oop, any $5.00-15.00
Betty Boop and Snow
   White $10.00-15.00
Big Chief Wahoo, any . . $5.00-7.50
Blondie and Dagwood,
   any $10.00-15.00
Buck Jones in Night
   Riders $20.00-30.00
Buck Jones, all others $10.00-15.00
Bugs Bunny, (first) . . . $17.50-30.00

Big Little Books from the "Golden Age". Walter Lantz's Andy Panda, $10.00-$15.00; Terry and the Pirates, $12.00-15.00; Bugs Bunny, $12.00-17.00 each; Buck Rogers, $22.00-27.50.

Bugs Bunny, all others $12.00-17.50
Captain Easy, any $5.00-10.00
Captain Midnight,
   any $12.00-15.00
Chester Gump, any .. $10.00-12.00
Dan Dunn, Secret Operative 48,
   1934 .... $20.00-25.00
Dan Dunn, any other .. $7.00-10.00
Dick Tracy, Detective and Federal
   Agent $25.00-30.00
Adventures of Dick
   Tracy $30.00-35.00
Dick Tracy, Frozen Bullet
   Murders $25.00-30.00
DIck Tracy, Maroon Mask
   Gang $25.00-30.00
Dick Tracy, Mystery of the
   Purple Cross $35.00-45.00
Dick Tracy, all others $15.00-25.00
Don Winslow, any $5.00-7.50
Donald Duck and the
   Ducklings $35.00-40.00
Donald Duck, all
   others $15.00-20.00
Ellery Queen, any $10.00-15.00
Felix the Cat, any $7.50-12.50
Flash Gordon on Planet
   Mongo $35.00-50.00
Flash Gordon, all
   others $30.00-40.00
G-Man, any $10.00-15.00
Gene Autry in
   Gunsmoke $25.00-35.00
Gene Autry, all others $12.50-17.50
Jungle Jim, any $12.50-17.50
King of the Royal
   Mounted $7.50-10.00
Little Orphan Annie,
   (first) $25.00-30.00
Little Orphan Annie, any
   other $17.50-22.00
Mickey Mouse, (first) $40.00-50.00
Mickey Mouse, all
   others $17.50-37.50

Popeye, any $12.50-17.50
Roy Rogers, any $10.00-15.00
Tarzan of the Apes ... $25.00-35.00
Tarzan, all others $7.50-10.00
Woody Woodpecker, Big Game
Hunter $10.00-15.00

Blue and White Pottery

Blue and white pottery or crockery is sometimes called blue & grey crockery, salt glaze, or blue and grey pottery. The blue and white crockery pitchers, salt holders, bowls and miscellaneous pieces were very popular in the United States from the late 1800's into the 1930's. Though there are some stenciled designs, most decoration is in the form of embossings. Prices are climbing upward on this collectible.

Pitchers

Standing deer and
fawn $60.00-75.00
Castle $55.00-70.00
Lincoln & cabin .... $150.00+
Poinsetta $70.00-85.00
Daisy $80.00-90.00
Grape $50.00-65.00
Windmill $50.00-75.00
Cow (small size) .... $115.00+
Pine cone $80.00-100.00
Indian boy & girl ... $75.00-100.00
Apple blossom $60.00-80.00
Cattail (small size) ... $45.00-60.00
Cattail (large size).... $45.00-60.00
Beaded rose $60.00-80.00
Cosmos $60.00-80.00
Cherry band $45.00-70.00
Lincoln .... $150.00+
Geometric design $60.00-75.00
Eagle .... $125.00+
Path & trees $50.00-70.00
Dutch boy & girl $60.00-80.00
Barrel $50.00-70.00
Dutch scene $45.00-50.00
Banded scroll $40.00-60.00
Apricot $50.00-70.00
Acorn $45.00-70.00

Columns $70.00-85.00
Tulip $70.00-80.00
Butterfly $70.00-80.00
Rose trellis......... $55.00-70.00
Love birds .... $100.00+
Jumping deer $80.00-100.00
Rose $60.00-80.00
Rose with band $65.00-80.00
Swan $85.00-100.00
Beaded swirl $60.00-80.00
Stupid pitcher $50.00-70.00
Dainty fruit $70.00-90.00

Salts

Plain salt $50.00-65.00
Waffle weave $50.00-70.00
Raspberry $50.00-70.00
Apple blossom $60.00-80.00
Eagle $80.00-100.00
Butterfly $60.00-80.00
Peacock $60.00-80.00
Oak leaf $50.00-70.00
Basket weave, tall $70.00-85.00
Grape & waffle $50.00-70.00
Love bird $80.00-100.00
Good luck sign $50.00-60.00
Grape & lattice $50.00-60.00
Grape & basket weave $50.00-60.00
Apricot $55.00-70.00
Daisy $50.00-70.00

Bowls

Love bird $60.00-70.00
Greek key $35.00-50.00
Cosmos $40.00-50.00
Pyramid........... $30.00-40.00
Apple blossom $40.00-50.00
Plain $30.00-40.00
Daisy $30.00-40.00
Diamond point $30.00-40.00

Butters

Butterfly $50.00-70.00
Apricot $55.00-75.00
Eagle with bird .... $150.00+
Dragon fly $60.00-80.00
Basket weave....... $50.00-70.00
Farm scene $70.00-85.00
Indian with deer ...... $115.00+

49

Blue & white stoneware pitchers. Advertising $75.00-100.00; Grape $50.00-70.00; Swirl, $50.00-70.00; Plain, $40.00-60.00; Girl and dog, $125.00 + .

Blue & white stoneware. Windmill, $50.00-60.00; Dutch boy, girl, and dog, $50.00-60.00; Barrel, $55.00-70.00; windmill,$50.00-60.00; Dutch scene, $55.00-70.00; Plain pitcher, $40.00-60.00.

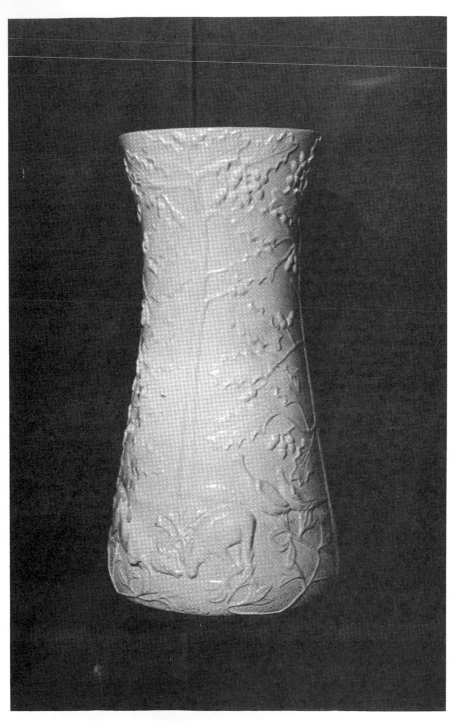

Blue and white Umbrella stand, $325.00.

Apple blossom water cooler, $300.00.

Blue Ridge Dinnerware

Southern Potteries' Blue Ridge Dinnerware is made up of a combination of pattern shapes and pattern decoration designs. Most collectible Blue Ridge consists of the dinnerware and accessories.

Ashtrays $1.00-2.00
Bowl, divided vegetable $6.00-10.00
Bowl, flat soup $2.00-4.00
Box, cigarette $4.00-7.00
Butter dish, ¼ lb....... $7.00-10.00
Carafe with lid $6.00-10.00

Child's mug $4.00-6.00
Cup $2.50-4.00
Dish, casserole $3.00-5.00
Gravy boat $4.00-9.00
Character jugs $50.00
Plate, dinner $2.00-4.50
Plate, pie $2.00-3.50
Plate, salad $1.50-3.50
Platter, 15'' $6.00-10.00
Salad fork $4.00-8.00
Saucer $1.25-2.50
Tea pot $10.00-17.00
Vase, handled $10.00-14.00
Vase, round $10.00-12.00

A group of Blue Ridge salt and pepper shakers. Each pair is worth about $8.00-10.00.

54

Blue Ridge chocolate pots. Left to right: Easter Parade, Rose Marie, French Peasant, Chintz. These are valued at $20.00 each.

Bottles

Bottles hold a fascination for many collectors. The first were crude containers holding whiskey, bitters, and other liquids. Gradually, improvements were made in the manufacturing processes of bottles and sealing methods. Liquor bottles, flasks, medicine bottles, soda bottles, beer bottles, and ink bottles are generally the most collected. The collecter should be on the lookout for reproduction and re-issue bottles.

These Bromo Seltzer bottles are worth about 1.00-3.00.

Bitters

Abbots, round, amber . . $2.00-6.00
Eagle Aromatic Bitters,
    amber $15.00-30.00
Dr. Fisch's Bitters,
    fish shape . . . . $125.00 +
Hentz Curative Bitters $40.00-60.00
Jeune Wine Bitters . . . $10.00-20.00
Pochontas Bitters,
    barrel shape $60.00-100.00
U.S. Gold Bitters,
    aqua $40.00-80.00
Rush's Bitters $25.00-50.00
Stag Bitters $4.00-10.00
Star Anchor Bitters . . $50.00-75.00

Three poison bottles with embossing on the side, $5.00-10.00 each.

Food

Mrs. Winslow's Syrup,
    figural $4.00-6.00
Mellins Infant Food $3.00-4.00
Queen Olives $4.00-10.00
Sauer's Extracts, cork . . $2.00-3.00
Whitehouse Vinegar . . . $6.00-10.00
Red Snapper Sauce $2.00-3.00
OK Sweet Pickles $4.00-6.00
Knights Extracts $1.00-2.00
Charles Gulden Mustard $1.00-2.00
Climax Seasoning $3.00-6.00

Poisons

Cobolt Owl Poison . . . $10.00-25.00
Poison Tinct Iodine $4.00-6.00
Poison, skull figural . . . . $100.00 +

Triloids Poison $8.00-10.00
Odos, Milk glass $10.00-20.00

Two figural food bottles. At left is a Grapette clown valued at $5.00-10.00. At right is a clock that held mustard, $5.00-10.00.

Cosmetics

American Lilac
    Perfume $8.00-15.00
Calders Dentine $1.00-2.00
Clairs Hair Lotion $6.00-10.00
New Brothers Herpicide $2.00-4.00
Reven Gloss Shoe
    Dressing $4.00-6.00

Medicine

Allens Lung Balm $6.00-10.00
Arnica & Oil Liniment . . $2.00-3.00
Bason Medicine Co. . . . $4.00-10.00
Bulls Herbs & Iron $6.00-16.00
Cod Liver Oil, embossed
    fish $4.00-12.00

Boxes

Boxes of wood, cardboard, and other materials are plentiful and though there are exceptions, many can be bought very reasonably. Look for Shaker boxes, small wood boxes and product containers.

Shaker boxes, round, wood,
    painted $250.00-400.00

Factory pantry box, similar to above without finger lapping $45.00-60.00

Seed boxes, Shaker, wood, multi-colored label $250.00-550.00

Austin & Graves Biscuits, wood, paper label $50.00-60.00

Document box, pine, dovetailed corners $25.00-30.00

Sewing box, Amish . . . . . $200.00+

Cracker box, Fox Bakery, wood $45.00-50.00

Quaker Oats, cylinder, cardboard, early $10.00-12.00

Thread box, Charter Oak, wood $15.00-20.00

Cereal box, Kellogg's Corn Flakes, cardboard, 6 x 8, early $15.00-20.00

Collar box, Pioneer Collar, cabin shape, cardboard $50.00-60.00

Grandpa's Wonder Soap, wood, paper label $30.00-35.00

Pepper box, R.S. Janney, cylinder, wood, paper label $65.00-70.00

Mason's Blacking, wood, paper label $20.00-25.00

Seed box, Lake Shore Seeds, wood compartments $40.00-50.00

Chalk box, wood $5.00-10.00

Irvin S. Cobb cigar box, paper and cardboard, $5.00-10.00

Wood boxes, left to right: optical lens box, $2.00-5.00; tobacco box, $5.00-10.00; cylindrical boxes, $2.00 each.

Butter Molds

Butter molds or butter prints are round, rectangular, or square forms for molding and imprinting designs on butter. Though most are made of wood, some can be found in metal glass, or other materials. The most common impressions on the molds are wheat, acorns, pineapples, and some floral designs. Most any animal impression is considered valuable, especially cows or deer. Beware of reproduction butter molds that are sometimes dificult to determine from the originals.

Wheat $45.00-50.00
Acorn.............. $30.00-35.00
Daisy $35.00-40.00
Double acorn $35.00-40.00
Rectangle, cherries ... $60.00-75.00
Eagle $150.00-175.00

Square, dovetailed, wooden, no impression $7.50-10.00

A square family mold with initials "R.L.", $175.00 + .

The swan, like other animals and birds, is somewhat rare among butter mold impressions. This example is worth about $50.00-65.00.

This early wheat box type mold is **valued at $50.00 to $60.00.**

Fern $30.00-35.00
Rectangle, double star $30.00-40.00
Grapes $40.00-50.00
Rooster $125.00-135.00
Sheep $150.00-170.00
Sunflower $60.00-75.00

Rectangle, wooden,
  no impression $7.50-10.00
Maple leaf $32.00-37.00
Pineapple $30.00-35.00
Tulip $75.00-85.00
Strawberry $45.00-55.00

A Pennsylvania Tulip adorns the **will bring as much as $100.00 or**
print of this mold. This rare design **more.**

Campaign Buttons

The first pinback buttons were used in the election of 1896. Their popularity has continued and they are still an effective means of candidate advertisement today. Early buttons were colorful, followed by a trend in the 30's and 40's toward red, white and blue. During this period most of the candidates buttons were very similiar. In later years the trend seems to be going back to more colorful buttons once again. The most popular buttons are jugates, buttons that feature both the presidential and vice presidential candidates. The collector should be very careful in purchasing political buttons. Many reproductions, especially of the earlier and more valuable buttons, are floating around.

(Photo courtesy of Hake's Americana & Collectibles)
A group of political buttons, from World War II to 1972. Top row from left: Roosevelt 1944, $8.00; Dewey 1944, $7.50; Truman 1948, $12.00; Dewey 1948, $7.50; Eisenhower 1952, $7.50; Stevenson 1952, $7.50; Second row from left: Eisenhower 1956, $3.50; Stevenson 1956, $3.00; Kennedy 1960, $5.00; Nixon and Lodge 1960 jugate, $5.00; Johnson 1964, $3.00; Goldwater 1964, $3.00. Bottom row from left: Nixon 1968, $2.00; Humphrey and Muskie 1968, $2.50; Wallace 1968, $1.00-1.50; Nixon 1972, $1.50; McGovern and Shriver, 1972, $1.00; McGovern and Eagleton 1972, $2.50.

(Photo courtesy of Hake's Americana & Collectibles)
A group of early political pinback buttons. Top row from left, McKinley,
1896, $10.00; Bryan 1896, $10.00; McKinley and Roosevelt jugate 1900,
$15.00; Bryan and Stevenson jugate 1900, $20.00; Roosevelt and Fairbanks
jugate 1904, $15.00; Parker and Davis jugate 1904, $15.00. Second row
from left: Taft 1908, $10.00; Bryan 1908, $12.00; Wilson and Marshall
jugate, 1912, $25.00; Taft and Sherman jugate 1912, $30.00; Roosevelt
(Bull Moose) 1912, $10.00; Wilson and Marshall jugate 1916, $25.00;
Hughes 1916, $15.00. Third row from left: Harding 1920, $10.00; Cox and
Roosevelt, 1920, $30.00; Coolidge 1924, $20.00; La Follette and Wheeler
1924, $10.00; Hoover 1928, $20.00; Smith 1928, $20.00; Bottom row from
left: Roosevelt 1932, $10.00; Hoover 1932, $10.00; Roosevelt and Garner
jugate 1936, $10.00; Landon 1936, $20.00; Roosevelt 1940, $7.50; Willkie
1940, $7.50.

Campaign Collectibles

Campaign collectibles are popular "go withs" for political button collections, and more recently in their own right as collectibles. The historical value combined with the wide variety of collectibles available make this collecting hobby one that offers many opportunities. Anything used as a campaign item is considered collectible, especially material from early campaigns. Be cautious in buying political collectibles to avoid reproductions on the market.

Bubble gum cigar, Win
  with HHH $1.00
Postcard, Nebraska
  for Taft $15.00
Watch fob, bronze, Bryan & Kern,
  1908 .... $15.00-20.00
Watch fob, Roosevelt,
  celluloid and metal,
  1940 .... $20.00-25.00
Poster, Harding & Coolidge,
  1920, 16x14 .... $30.00-35.00
Poster, Thomas Dewey,
  18 x 24 .... $7.50-10.00
Folding lantern, Grant
  & Wilson .... $200.00 +

President Nixon.
Now more than ever.

Shopping bag from 1972 campaign.

Cap, paper, Goldwater & Miller,
1964 . . . . $10.00-12.00
Cup, paper,
Eisenhower $7.00-10.00
Bandana, silk, Woodrow
Wilson $17.00-20.00
Matchbook, Nixon, 1972 . . . . $2.00
Mug, Hoover, ceramic $100.00

Mug, F.D. Roosevelt . $25.00-27.50
Handkerchief, McKinley
& Hobart $60.00-70.00
Poster, Windell Wilke $15.00-20.00
Lantern, McKinley &
Roosevelt . . . . $175.00 +
Pennant, Eisenhower &
Nixon, 1952 . . . . $12.00-15.00

FREE INSIDE: NEW, GIANT FOLD-OUT POSTER FOR YOUR WALL.

Campaign literature from the 1972   Nixon-McGovern race.

63

Fan, Horace Greely,
paper $50.00-75.00
Cane, Taft, silverplate
head $40.00-50.00
Cigar, McGovern, 10" $7.00-10.00
Goblet, Grant & Wilson,
1872 .... $200.00+
License plate, Hoover $20.00-25.00
Pocket knife, T.
Roosevelt......... $50.00-60.00
Lapel stud, McKinley,
silver .... $100.00+
Thimble, Coolidge &
Dawes $10.00-15.00
Ring, Hoover, 1928 .. $17.00-20.00
Plate, McKinley $25.00-30.00
Pennant, Kennedy & Johnson,
1960 .... $5.00-6.50

Candy Containers

Figural containers of glass first became popular in the 19th century. The idea was to boost the sale of candy by packaging it in a container that could later be used as a toy. This was so successful that many manufacturers adopted the idea in the years following and packaged many products in the attractive containers. The collector should beware because some of the figural containers are still being produced or are currently being reproduced.

Betty Boop $25.00-27.00
Rabbit and baby $75.00-100.00
Rabbit sitting on
cracked egg $50.00-55.00
Babe Ruth ballplayer . $40.00-50.00
Trolley .... $75.00+
Mail box $20.00-25.00
Charlie Chaplin
and jar $75.00-85.00
Jackie Coogan, "The Kid .... Rare
Zeppelin $25.00-35.00
Spirit of St. Louis $60.00-75.00

The rabbit, chick and swan boat will   bring about $40.00.

Large barrel $40.00-45.00
Hatching chick in car . $40.00-45.00
Happy Time alarm clock $5.00-7.00
World War I tank $35.00-40.00
Barney Google .... Rare
Sparkplug $45.00-55.00
Eiffel Tower $10.00-15.00
Ice Truck $30.00-35.00
Pig standing $6.00-8.00
Cannon, cobalt blue .. $40.00-50.00
Felix the cat, on circus tub ... Rare
Uncle Sam hat $30.00-40.00

Carnival Glass

Carnival Glass was originally called Taffeta, but because it was a popular give-away at carnivals it came to be called Carnival Glass. Large quantities were produced from about 1900 to the 1930's but some manufacturers are still manufacturing the popular glassware. Carnival Glass is an iridized glass that has a "rainbow" effect when under sunlight. Many patterns were produced in several colors and many pieces are signed. The most popular makers of Carnival Glass were Millersburg, Northwood, and Fenton. The collector should be very cautious when buying Carnival Glass because many pieces are being made today.

Northwood Springtime pitcher and two tumbler worth about $675.00 for the

Imperial Open Rose plate, $50.00.

Acorn, plate 9'', dark ... $200.00 +
Apple Blossom, bowl, 7'',
   marigold $7.00-10.00
Basketweave & Cable, creamer,
   marigold $20.00-30.00
Bird & Grapes, wall vase,
   marigold $30.00-40.00
Bo-Peep, plate, dark . $70.00-85.00
Feather Scroll, tumbler,
   dark $20.00-30.00
Fern, compote, dark . $10.00-20.00
Flute, tumbler $20.00-40.00
Gooseberry Spray, bowl,
   5'' $10.00-30.00
Harvest Flower,
   tumbler $40.00-80.00
Honeycomb, rose bowl . $100.00 +
Inverted Coin Dot,
   pitcher $125.00-250.00
Jeweled Heart, plate
   7'' $20.00-30.00

Kokomo, rose bowl .. $30.00-60.00
Lattice & Daisy,
   tumbler $15.00-30.00
Mayan, bowl, 9'' $20.00-40.00
Northern Star, bon bon $5.00-10.00
Octagon, goblet $15.00-25.00
Split Diamond,
   creamer $20.00-30.00
Star & Fan, vase $70.00-80.00
Stippled Petals, bowl . $50.00-60.00
Strawberry, plate 9'' . $50.00-85.00
Swirl, bowl, 7'' $15.00-25.00
Thistle & Thorn,
   creamer $20.00-30.00
Tiger Lily, pitcher .. $90.00-150.00
Trout & Fly, square
   bowl .... $175.00 +
Vintage, powder jar .. $25.00-35.00
Woodpecker, wall
   vase .... $800.00 +
Zippered Heart, vase ... $800.00 +

Catalogs

One of the most popular sales aids in this country for many years has been the trade catalog. Through the collecting of these catalogs, the collector can witness the types of things bought by the American public over the years. Some catalog collectors specialize in a particular company and try to accumulate catalogs for that company only. Others "zero in" on a specific type of merchandise and look for catalogs from companies that produced only this merchandise. Still others collect a complete cross-section of many companies for many years. At any rate, catalog collecting is growing as more and more collectors "discover" these collectibles. be very careful in this area, because many of the old trade catalogs are being reproduced.

D.M. Ferry catalog, 1885, $15.00-20.00.

Charles Williams, clothing,
   1915 . . . . $12.00-17.00
Bedell, clothing, 1914 . . $5.00-7.00
Gimbell Holiday Book,
   1903 . . . . $10.00-15.00

Marbles Outing Equipment,
   1925 . . . . $10.00-15.00
Nater Homes & Garages,
   1920's $2.50-5.00
Montgomery Ward Spring Supple-
   ment, 1913 . . . . $5.00-7.50
Boston Trading Company,
   camping, etc., 1930's . $5.00-7.50

St. Johns Tables, 1922, $5.00-10.00.

Stetson Steps, ladies shoes,
   1920's $2.00-4.00
Whitall Tatum & Co., laboratory
   glassware, 1890's . . $10.00-12.00
Stanley Rule & Level Company,
   1890's $25.00-30.00
Colt Firearms, Law & Order
   Division, 1930's . . . $35.00-40.00
Larkin Co., 1911-12,
   general $15.00-17.50
Honor Bilt Modern Homes,
   Sears, 1928 . . . . $2.50-5.00
Old Town Canoes,
   1920's $5.00-7.50
Savage Arms, 1938 . . . $10.00-12.50
Westinghouse Electric Co.,
   Industrial lighting,
   1931 . . . . $2.50-4.00
Elias Howe Company, Musical
   Instruments, 1890's $10.00-12.00
J.D. Warren Co., hardware store
   fixtures, 1900's $10.00-15.00

A.C. Gilbert Co., toy trains,
   1930's $20.00-25.00
Lionel, trains, 1939 . . $20.00-25.00

Weiller & Son Jewelry catalog from 1917 worth about $15.00.

Character Collectibles

The popularity of comic characters and movie, radio, and T.V. characters has produced an onslaught of toys, games, books, lamps, dishes, and hundreds of other types of memorabilia. Anything named after the character, featuring his likeness, or remotely connected to the caracter is considered collectible. Most sought after items are those produced from the 1920's to the early 1950's, but some items of more recent production are becoming increasingly valuable. Early items of still popular characters generally are the most valuable.

Roy Rogers bowl $15.00-17.50
Gene Autry belt
   and buckle $15.00-17.00

Flash Gordon gun,
   1930's . . . . $100.00 +
Felix the Cat, wood,
   cat in car $65.00-75.00
Buck Rogers Battle Cruiser,
   Tootsietoy $25.00-35.00
Donald Duck, drummer, tin wind-
   up, Marx $40.00-45.00
Captain Midnight,
   membership token,
   1940's . . . . $.50-6.00
Mighty Mouse, 9'',
   rubber figure $5.00-10.00
Dick Tracy Squad Car, 1940's
   metal with plastic
   figures $25.00-35.00
Elmer Fudd hand puppet,
   1950's $2.00-3.00
Happy Hooligan donkey cart,
   1920's $125.00-150.00
Jiggs stick puppet,
   12'' $20.00-30.00
Lil' Abner & Dogpatch Band,
   tin, 1940's . . . . $150.00 +
Howdy Doody puppet, 1950's,
   cardboard $5.00-7.50
Lone Ranger glow-in-the-dark
   belt, 1940's $25.00-35.00
Orphan Annie Bandana,
   1930's $20.00-30.00

Tom Mix Decoder Badge, $25.00.

A group of character figures and puppets produced by the Shoenhut Toy Co. Felix the cat, $100.00; Boob McNutt, $300.00; Maggie and Jiggs, $400.00; Happy Hooligan $200.00; Barney Google and Sparkplug, $300.00.

Sky King, Aztec Indian
   Ring $25.00-35.00
Superman Crusader
   Ring $35.00-50.00
Tom Mix manual,
   1944 . . . . $25.00-35.00
Wild Bill Hickock Treasure Map,
   1950's, Kellogg's . . $15.00-25.00
Heckle & Jeckle squeeze toys,
   1950's $5.00-7.50
Orphan Annie stove,
   metal, 1930's $15.00-25.00
Popeye doll, 20"
   1950's $10.00-15.00
Porky Pig squeeze toy,
   6" 1940's $5.00-10.00
Red Ryder Target Game,
   1930's $18.00-25.00

Sgt. Preston Trail Kit . $30.00-50.00

Tom Mix whistle ring, $25.00.

Tarzan mask, 1930's . $25.00-35.00
Deputy Dawg doll,
  1960's $10.00-15.00
Hopalong Cassidy dart board,
  1950 . . . . $5.00-7.50
Matt Dillon U.S. Marshall
  badge $2.00-3.00

Children's Dishes

Most of the major glass producers in this country around the turn of the century and before produced a line of miniature pattern dishes for children. These dishes have an excellent quality, clear patterns and are, many times, small versions of patterns found in large pieces. Children's glassware has recently enjoyed an increased following and popular pieces of high quality are demanding high prices. Be careful to avoid reproductions.

Creamer, Bead &
  Scroll $40.00-50.00
Sugar, Beaded Swirl . . $25.00-35.00
Cake plate, Champion $40.00-50.00
Butter, Clambroth . . . $60.00-80.00
Creamer, Cloud Band $60.00-75.00
Tumbler, Colonial $7.50-10.00
Water pitcher,
  Portland $25.00-35.00
Tumbler, Portland . . . $12.00-15.00
Mug, Drum $25.00-30.00
Butter, Drum $80.00-100.00
Large berry, Flute . . . $25.00-30.00
Butter, Block &
  Rosette $45.00-50.00
Spooner, Button
  Panel $35.00-45.00
Butter, Buzzsaw $30.00-35.00
Punch bowl, Cambridge Wheat
  Sheaf $30.00-35.00
Small berry, Flute $7.50-10.00
Cake plate, Hawaiian
  Lei $25.00-30.00

A grouping of children's dishes in the "Pert" pattern. The pieces here are a covered sugar bowl, **$45.00-60.00; covered butter dish, $50.00-65.00; creamer, $35.00-45.00; spooner $35.00-45.00.**

Punch bowl set of the Flattened Sunburst pattern. The punch set is valued at $100.00.

Tray, Hobnail
    Thumbprint $30.00-35.00
Small bowl, Lacy Daisy $7.50-10.00
Spooner, Lamb...... $65.00-75.00
Mug, Liberty Bell ..... $100.00 +
Creamer, Lion $60.00-75.00

Civil War Collectibles

Items used in the War Between the States have not only a monetary value but also a great historic value. If the collector unearths the item himself, he should trace it to the best of his ability and keep careful records of the finding place. This not only makes the item more interesting, but an item complete with its history is more valuable. The collector should take such caution, because of many of the items used in the Civil War are being reproduced, especially buckles, bullets, decorations, swords, guns and more. Prices can vary greatly on Civil War memorabilia due to the historical nature.

Saddlebags, leather,
    marked U.S. $95.00-115.00
Saddle, wood &
    buckskin............ $100.00 +
Pistol cartridge box & cap box,
    leather $25.00-35.00
Telegraph spool,
    confederate .... $150.00 +
Canteen, leather $20.00-25.00
Map case, wood $40.00-70.00
Holster with flap for revolver,
    leather $25.00-30.00
Field surgeon's kit, amputating
    & operating instruments in
    large wood case ...... $750.00 +
Calvary hat, Union ..... $100.00 +
Calvary hat, Confederate $100.00 +

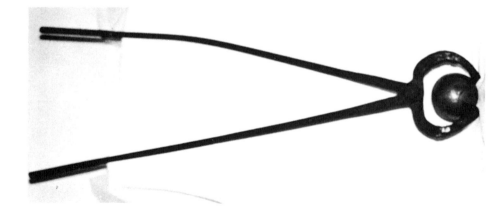

Is t d by the Richmond & Danville R. R. Co. on the Requisition

SOLDIER'S TICKET.

No. _____ | FROM

_____ Seats | TO

Of the Quartermaster's Department of the Confederate States

This Ticket is issued on a requisition of the Assistant Quartermaster of the Confederate States at Richmond, Va., and will be paid for by the Confederate States, upon presenting this coupon.

A soldiers pass from the Richmond & Danville Railroad for use by a Confederate soldier. Rare.

These cannonball tongs from a Civil War factory in Pennsylvania are worth about $50.00.

Daguerreotype, soldier,
  Confederate, small . $25.00-35.00
Officers coat, Union . $60.00-80.00
Brass buckle, Eagle .. $25.00-35.00
Mess kit $20.00-25.00
Drum .... $200.00 +
Officers sword .... $175.00 +
Bayonet & Scarbard,
  Confederate $40.00-50.00
Telescope, brass ...... $200.00 +
Calvary spurs,
  Confederate........ $150.00 +
Powder keg $35.00-50.00

Clocks

Clock collecting has been a major pastime of collectors for a number of years. There are many variations of clocks: wall clocks, mantle clocks, kitchen clocks, novelty clocks, grandfather clocks. They have been manufactured through the years in a number of woods and styles. Most popular with collectors are clocks made by the large clock companies: Seth Thomas, Waterbury, Ithaca, Ingraham, Welch,

Wall clocks. Ithaca calendar No. 4 $1200.00; Seth Thomas Regulator No. 8 $400.00; Seth Thomas Drop Octagon $250.00.

Gilbert mantel clocks. The Bonan-
za, top and the Major from about
1900, $125.00 each.

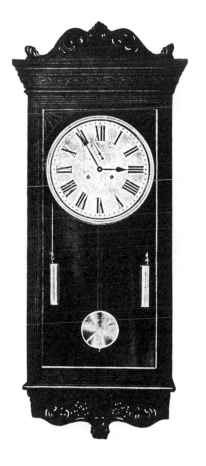
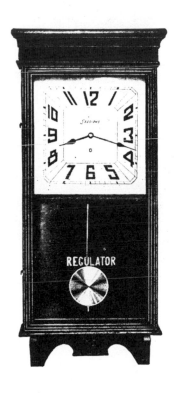

Two Sessions wall Regulators from about 1930. The Regulator #2 above is worth about $200.00, the

Regulator #3 below could bring as much as $750.00 or more.

Sessions, and Ansonia are only a few. Prices here are for clocks that have been completely restored and in good working condition.

Seth Thomas, dresser, night
 clock A $30.00-40.00
Seth Thomas, mantle, Fleet #15,
 1910 .... $115.00-125.00
Seth Thomas, mantle, Pequod,
 1905 .... $80.00-90.00
Seth Thomas, mantle, Pasha,
 1905 .... $80.00-90.00
Seth Thomas, weight, O.G.,
 1885 .... $85.00-95.00

Seth Thomas, weight, Column,
 1885 .... $300.00+
Seth Thomas, spring, Office #2,
 1880's .... $200.00+
Seth Thomas, spring, Office
 Calendar #6 .... $2500.00+
Seth Thomas, hall clock, #27,
 1905 .... $50000.00+
Seth Thomas, weight, Regulator
 #18, 1885 .... $1300.00
Waterbury, lever, R.C. Octagon,
 1880 .... $120.00-130.00
Waterbury, wall, Drop
 Octagon, 1918 .... $200.00+

Waterbury, wall, Andes,
1918 . . . . $200.00 +

Waterbury, novelty, Agout,
1918 . . . . $35.00-40.00

Waterbury, kitchen, #9093,
1930 . . . . $150.00 +

Waterbury, wall, Fostoria,
1918 . . . . $400.00 +

Waterbury, mantel, Edmond,
1918 . . . . $60.00-70.00

Waterbury, mantel, Eagle,
1918 . . . . $60.00-70.00

Waterbury, weight, O.O.G.,
1880 . . . . $125.00 +

Waterbury, mantel, Florence,
1880 . . . . $100.00 +

Ansonia, novelty, Midget,
1886 . . . . $40.00-50.00

Ansonia, mantel, Arcadian,
1886 . . . . $150.00 +

Ansonia, mantel, Standard,
1886 . . . . $150.00

Ansonia, mantel, King,
1886 . . . . $200.00 +

Ansonia, mantel, Kentucky,
1886 . . . . $175.00 +

New Haven, Mission Hanging,
1918 . . . . $150.00 +

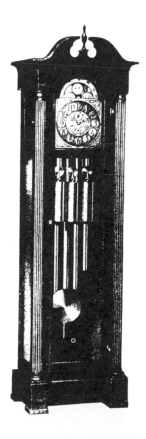

Most hall or grandfather clocks cost several thousand dollars. This example, a Sessions #9003 is valued at about $3000.00.

Waterbury Pontiac $400.00.

Howard, wall, #36, Regulator,
1880 . . . . $5000.00 +

Howard, wall, #70,
1880 . . . . $1000.00 +

Ingraham, mantel, Meteor,
1930 . . . . $30.00-40.00

Ingraham, Banjo, Nile,
1930 . . . . $275.00 +

Ingraham, mantel, Pekin,
1918 . . . . $65.00-75.00

Coca-Cola Bottles

With the increased interest in collecting Coca-Cola advertising material there has also been a rise in value and interest in collecting Coke bottles. Over the years, the Coca-Cola bottle has evolved from a plain thick bottle with a stopper to a streamlined, easy to hold container. Coke bottlers have been located in many

Giant display bottle from Mexico, made in the late 1960's. White on aqua, 20½" tall, $20.00-25.00.

Giant display bottle dated December 25, 1923, 20½" tall, embossed on aqua, $100.00.

Coca-Cola bottles from the Biedenharn Candy Co., Vicksburg, Mississippi, one of the first Coke bottlers. The Hutchinson bottle at left is the earliest bottle to carry Coke, but because it was used to carry other beverages is not the most valuable Coke bottle. It is worth about $50.00-60.00. The other bottles in the photograph are valued at $15.00-25.00.

Left is an unusual shouldered bottle from Columbus, Ohio with Coca-Cola in script worth about $12.00. Three middle bottles are variations of Coke bottles from Birmingham, Chicago, and Tampa and are worth about $10.00 each. At right is a paper label Coke bottle worth around $12.00.

Foreign Coke bottles. Left to right: Tel Aviv, Japan, Taipei, Taipei. $10.00 each.

More foreign Coca-Cola bottles. Left to right: Canada, $10.00; Spain, Mexico, and Canada, $5.00-7.00 each.

Coke bottle variations containing Coca-Cola script. The two on the left are worth about $10.00 or more. The odd shaped bottle is valued at $20.00. the bottle on the right is the first Mae West or contoured bottle, marked Nov. 16, 1915, $10.00.

parts of the country and for a number of years there was no standard bottle for the beverage. These two points combined offer the collector many examples to include in a collection. Bottles in bad condition are generally not collectible, unless they are extremely rare. Bottles that have the original paper labels are worth more than the same type without the label. Many anniversary and commemorative bottles have been produced recently in the style of earlier bottles, so the collector should beware.

Coca-Cola Collectibles

The success of Coca-Cola has provided American collectors with both a challenging and profitable hobby. Because of the extensive use of advertising Coca-Cola authorized production of great numbers of items to be given away as premiums and sold as promotion. Anything produced in the early 1900's is in great demand. Caution should be taken in this area because many of the more popular and valuable collectibles are being produced.

Toy truck, original bottles,
    1920's . . . . $125.00 +
Bookmark, Lillian Nordica,
    1903 . . . . $100.00 +
Window bottle holder, metal,
    1940's $30.00-35.00
Lighter, miniature bottle,
    1950's $5.00-7.50
Carton, wood, bail handle,
    1930's $25.00-35.00
Carton, metal, bail handle,
    1940's $20.00-25.00
Circus set, cardboard
    cutouts $35.00-50.00

A cardboard stand-up Santa Claus advertisement from 1953 stands about 18" high. It is valued today at $17.00-$25.00.

Hand fan, Coke bottle and hand,
1940's $12.00-15.00
Thermometer, tin silhouette of
girl drinking Coke . $30.00-35.00
Booklet, Pause for Living,
1960's $3.00-5.00
Bottle bags, paper,
1930's $3.00-5.00
Calendars, 1957,
flowers $12.00-15.00

An early Coca-Cola bottle opener, $10.00.

Billfold, leather,
1920's $35.00-37.50
Metal sign, girl holding bottle,
1926 . . . . $75.00-100.00
Ice pick, bottle opener, wood
handle, 1940 . . . . . . $7.50-10.00
Calendar, 1919, Marion
Davies $30.00-35.00
Door push, porcelain . $25.00-35.00
Coupon, "Good for free Coke"
1930's $5.00-6.00
Mirrored sign "Please Pay When
Served", round $75.00-90.00
Bottling Company letterhead,
early 1900's $10.00-20.00
Baseball bat, 1950's . . . . $100.00 +

A tin Coca-Cola thermometer from the early 1940's. $30.00-35.00.

Coca-Cola Trays

Trays, only one of many types of advertising items produced by Coca-Cola, continue to be very high on collector's want lists these days. The colorful attractive trays that have been in production since 1898 are demanding premium prices as more

The 1942 Coke tray, $25.00-40.00. The 1950 tray on the right, $12.00-17.00.

people begin to "discover" these images of American life. The changes in the characters and scenes on the trays reflect the changes in this country in fashion and social events. The prices here are for the large serving trays, rather than the small change trays that were generally small versions of the former. Be on the lookout for reproductions in this area because many are being sold today.

1898, round, girl with
glass .... $2500.00 +
1900, round, Coke bottle,
5¢ .... $750.00 +
1900, round, Hilda Clark $500.00 +
1904, round, Hilda Clark $500.00 +

1904, oval, St. Louis Fair and
girl $125.00-250.00
1904, smaller version of
above $100.00-200.00
1904, oval, Lillian Russell, glass
on table .... $500.00 +
1904, same as above with bottle
on table .... $500.00 +
1905, oval, girl drinking from
glass $125.00-250.00
1907, oval, girl holding
glass $150.00-300.00
1908-1912, Topless girl, advertising
on front .... $300.00 +
1908-1912, same as above,
advertising on
back $100.00-150.00

82

1908-1912, Vienna Art, four different, advertising on back $75.00-100.00

1909, oval, Coca-Cola Girl . . . . $250.00 +

1909, rectangle, same as above . . . . $225.00 +

1912, oval, girl with hat holding glass $125.00-250.00

1912, rectangle, same as above $100.00-150.00

1914, oval, "Betty" $175.00-200.00

1917, long rectangle, girl with roses holding glass . $50.00-85.00

1920, oval, girl in hat with glass $175.00-250.00

1920, rectangle, same as above $75.00-125.00

1921, rectangle, closeup of girl in hat holding glass . $100.00-125.00

1922, rectangle, girl with small hat under tree $200.00-250.00

1923, rectangle, girl in shawl $75.00-100.00

1924, rectangle, girl with glass $50.00-85.00

1925, rectangle, girl with fur and hat holding glass . . . $50.00-75.00

1926, rectangle, golfer pouring Coke for girl $50.00-85.00

1927, rectangle, soda jerk $45.00-75.00

The 1933 tray featuring Frances Dee, $50.00-75.00. The 1939 tray about $20.00-35.00.

1927, rectangle, car
hop $65.00-125.00
1930, girl in swimsuit &
cap $40.00-65.00
1931, rectangle, "Tom
Sawyer" $75.00-100.00
1932, rectangle, girl in chair wearing
swimsuit $75.00-125.00
1933, rectangle, Frances
Dee, ... $50.00-75.00
1934, rectangle, J. Weismuller &
M. O'Sullivan . . . $150.00-175.00
1935, rectangle, Madge
Evans $25.00-45.00
1936, rectangle, girl with long
gown on chair $35.00-50.00
1937, rectangle, girl in swimsuit
& cape running $25.00-50.00
1938, rectangle, girl in large
hat $25.00-40.00
1939, rectangle, girl in swimsuit on
diving board $20.00-35.00
1941, rectangle, girl in ice
skates $25.00-40.00
1942, rectangle, two girls and
car $25.00-40.00
1943, rectangle, girl with scarf
holding bottle $15.00-20.00
1950, rectangle, girl with hat
holding bottle $12.00-17.00
1956, rectangle with wavy edges,
party food $10.00-12.00

Collector Prints

Limited edition prints have become very popular with collectors in the past few years. Some signed and numbered limited edition prints, even though they are not old, bring considerably more than their original purchase prices. Prints by American artists Norman Rockwell, Charles Frace', Ray Harm and other noted wildlife artists are much in demand. Largely due to the limited production of these lithographs, the values appreciate rapidly on high quality prints. Prices here are for signed and numbered limited edition prints.

Harry Adamson, Winging in
Pintails . . . . $375.00 +
Harry Antis, American
Elk . . . . $45.00 +
Harry Antis, Timber
Wolf . . . . $100.00 +
Guy Coheleach, Golden
Eagle . . . . $300.00 +
Guy Coheleach, Snow
Leopard . . . . $200.00 +
Tom Dunnington, American
Bald Eagle . . . . $225.00 +
Eon Eckelberry, Barred
Owl . . . . $200.00 +
Bart Forbes,
Westward $35.00-50.00

Two prints by wildlife artist Ray Harm. The Bald Eagle is valued at about $300.00.

The Eagle and Osprey will bring as much as $2000.00.

84

Charles Frace', Snow
  Leopard . . . . $200.00 +
Charles Frace', Golden
  Eagle . . . . $100.00 +
Charles Frace', Elephants at
  Kilimanjaro . . . . $100.00 +
David Hagarbaumer, Foggy
  Morning Mallards . . . . $500.00 +
Ray Harm, Whitetail
  Deer . . . . $100.00 +
John Korver, Out of the
  Mist . . . . $90.00 +
David Maas, Winter Winds,
  Bluebills . . . . $175.00 +
Gordon Phillips, Tracks
  Snowed Under $85.00-95.00
Phil Prentice, Lion . . . $70.00-80.00
Maynard Reece, Wood
  Ducks . . . . $275.00 +
Arthur Singer, Pheasant $100.00 +

Comic Books

Comics have become more and more popular especially as the publicity of the hobby has increased. Collectors of all ages have swarmed to this new collectible that was once the domain of the youngster, causing a demand for some early rare books. The most popular valuable issues of comic books are those from the "Golden Age" that lasted from 1930 until 1950, especially the well known comic characters. Collectors are always on the lookout for issues containing the first appearance of a popular character. Some of these early examples can bring hundreds or even thousands of dollars to the alert seller. Comic books containing the work of Disney artist Carl Barks has also become very valuable in recent years. Though there are some very valuable comic books, most are still worth only a few cents each.

The Amazing Spiderman #3,
  early 1960's $25.00-50.00

Disney characters have been comic book favorites for a number of years. The MICKEY MOUSE BOOK from 1930 marks the first appearance of a Disney character in comic book form. A good copy of this comic can bring over $250.00. Pluto is another popular Disney character and this issue of MICKEY MOUSE MAGAZINE from the 1930's is worth about $35.00-$50.00.

Annie Oakley #1,
  1948 . . . . $12.00-17.50
Archie's Girls, Betty and Veronica
  #1, 1950 . . . . $25.00-50.00
Batman #3, features Cat
  Woman $150.00-275.00
Blondie Comics #1,
  1940's $5.00-10.00
Bugs Bunny and Porky Pig,
  1960's $1.00-3.00
Butch Cassidy and the Wild Bunch,
  1951 . . . . $10.00-12.00
Cisco Kid Comics, 1950 . $3.00-5.00
Colt 45, 1950's-1960's . . $1.25-2.50
Daredevil #1, 1964 . . . $35.00-50.00
Detective #27, Batman . $1000.00 +
Edgar Bergen Presents Charlie
  McCarthy, 1938 . . . $15.00-25.00
Fat and Slat, 1940's . . $10.00-20.00
Flash Gordon#1, 1950 $35.00-50.00
Herbie #1, 1960's $10.00-15.00
Howdy Doody #1,
  1940's $5.00-10.00
I Spy #1, 1960's $1.00-2.50

Looney Tunes and Merrie Melodies
#1, 1940's $125.00-250.00
Man From Uncle #1,
1960's.............. $1.00-3.00
Peter Rabbit, 1950's.... $2.00-4.00
Pogo Possum #1 .... $50.00-100.00
Sad Sack #1, 1940's .. $15.00-20.00
Star Trek #1, 1967 ... $10.00-12.50
Superboy #1, 1940's .... $200.00+
Torchy #1, 1940's ...... $150.00+
War Comics, 1950-1957 $2.00-10.00

Crockery

Crockery, also known as stoneware, pottery, and earthenware is made of clay that has been baked and glazed. The advantage of this kind of container was largely that the crock could keep cold materials cool for a longer period of time than glass bottles. Also, anything affected by light could be safely stored in the heavy opaque containers. The majority of pottery jars and jugs were made in the 1800's but many were produced more recently. Advertising crocks, crocks with a company's name or markings, are becoming very popular. The collector should be careful because it is often difficult to determine new from old crockery. One method to distinguish the difference is to find "turkey tracks", hairline age cracks in the interior or exterior of the jug. These cracks can also be reproduced, however, so extreme caution should be taken. Crockery with interior glaze was not produced until this century.

Apple butter pot, green glaze
redware $75.00-100.00
Cottage cheese mold, redware,
1800's........... $75.00-100.00
Pie plate, redware,
1800's........... $75.00-100.00
Wesson Oil advertising,
small $35.00-45.00

3 gallon, pear shape,
1840's.......... $275.00-300.00
Jug, J. & E. Norton, 1850's,
blue bird $250.00-300.00
Cylindrical, stenciled lettering,
Shaker $175.00-200.00
Pear shape jug, brown with blue
decoration, 1840's. S.
Risley $275.00-325.00
Jug, Bennington Vermont,
1870's.......... $150.00-200.00
Jar, C. W. Braun, Buffalo, New
York 1800's $300.00-350.00
Crock, 6 gallon, blue bird
decoration,
1860's.......... $300.00-375.00
Crock, Ottman Brothers, Fort
Edward, New York,
4 gallon $250.00-275.00

This two gallon jug with painted bird is from the New York Stoneware Company about 1870. It is valued at $225.00 or more.

wheel. The edges on the indentations of cut glass are sharper than on pieces of pressed glass. Signed glass, or those pieces with the company name or trademark are premium items and demand higher prices. The signature is made by a stamp that has been saturated with an acid solution. Prices here are for cut crystal in perfect condition. The collector should be especially careful of chips on cut glass and also reproduction glass that closely resembles the originals.

Cut glass vases, $40.00-60.00 each.

A two gallon stoneware jar with deep blue flower marked "Lyons". $175.00.

Pickling jar, 1½ gallon, 1850's
  decorated $150.00-175.00
Spittoon, decorated, early
  1800's $220.00-250.00
Butter crock, with wire
  bail $25.00-30.00
Liquor jug, C.S. Grove
  Co. $25.00-30.00

Cut Glass

Cut glass is extremely popular among collectors, especially those pieces produced during the period known as the "Brilliant Age", 1875-1915. Cut glass has a high lead content making it ring when thumped lightly and also causing it to have considerable weight. It is glass that has been hand blown and hand decorated with an abrasive

Handled basket, 8" . . . . $275.00 +
Handled basket, 6-7" . . . $150.00 +
Tea bell, 6" $135.00-150.00
Bon-bon $60.00-100.00
Butter dish, covered . . . . $250.00 +
Butterette, 3½" $25.00-40.00
Butter tub and plate
  open $175.00-200.00
Carafe, quart $125.00-150.00
Celery dip, 2" $20.00-40.00
Table salt, 2"x4" $15.00-30.00
Knife rest, 3½" $25.00-40.00
Celery tray, 12" . . . $125.00-150.00
Cheese plate, covered . . . $250.00 +
Whipped cream bowl, 3 handled
  6" $125.00-150.00
Mayonnaise set, 6" . $85.00-100.00
Cigar jar, 8½",
  covered . . . . $225.00 +

A cut glass water set will bring about $150.00 or more.

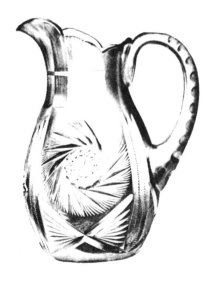

Creamer $50.00-70.00
Sugar, open $50.00-70.00
Cup $25.00-35.00
Cruet ⅓ pint $50.00-70.00
Decanters, 1 quart . . . . . . $200.00 +
Claret jug $170.00-200.00
Flemish jug . . . . $250.00 +
Whiskey flagon . . . . $200.00 +
Finger bowl, 5" $40.00-50.00

This three pint pitcher is worth about $160.00-180.00.

Cigar jar in oak frame . . $300.00 +
Tobacco jar, 7½" . . . . . . $275.00 +
Cologne bottle, 7" . . . $45.00-60.00
Comb & brush tray, 11" $250.00 +
Pomade box, 2¾" . . . $50.00-70.00
Pin tray $60.00-80.00

A half pint syrup of cut glass. Made by J.D. Bergen, this pitcher is valued at $35.00-$50.00 and is of the Oregon pattern.

Goblets	$45.00-60.00
Ice cream tray	$75.00-100.00
Sherbert	$100.00-125.00
Tea caddy	$100.00-125.00
Horse radish jar	$60.00-80.00
Pitcher	$200.00+
Nappie	$50.00-70.00
Puff box, 6"	$45.00-60.00
Hatpin holder, 7"	$50.00-70.00
Compote, 8"	$200.00+

A Glenwood sugar bowl made by J.D. Bergen. This excellent example of cut glass will bring $60.00-$80.00.

Decoys

Decoys have been used for many years to lure waterfowl to hunting areas. The decoys are wood turned or hand carved models of the fowl painted to resemble them and used to attract the birds into shooting range. The most valuable decoys are the early ones of wood, especially the more detailed ones. Prices can fluctuate due to quality of workmanship, condition, and rarity. Beware of modern reproductions.

Canada Goose, wood, hand carved & painted	$175.00-200.00
Canvasback, hen, wood	$40.00-55.00
Black Duck, wood, handmade	$50.00-65.00
Bluebill, wood	$25.00-30.00
Crow, wood	$35.00-40.00
Merganser, pair, painted	$200.00+
Raven, painted, handcarved	$1000.00+
Duck, paint removed	$15.00-20.00
Duck, cloth	$5.00-10.00
Snow Goose, handcarved wood	$60.00-75.00
Canvasback, cork	$15.00-25.00

A 15" wood duck with paint remov-   **ed, $15.00-20.00.**

This wood Black Duck is worth about $75.00-100.00.

Redhead, cork	$40.00-50.00
Golden Plover, cork	$15.00-25.00
Bluewing Teal, wood	$50.00-60.00
Broadbill, wood	$45.00-55.00
Golden Plover, wood	$40.00-50.00

Depression Glass

Depression glass is the glassware that was made during the years of the Depression, usually in pink, green, amber, blue, red, yellow,

Adam. Cup and saucer, $15.00; plate, $6.00; salt shaker, $35.00; sherbet, $10.00; coaster, $13.00; dessert bowl, $6.50.

American Pioneer. Sugar, $5.00;   plate, $4.00; ice bucket, $17.50.

Aunt Polly. Sugar bowl and cover, $3.00; butter dish and cover,
$35.00; 6'' plate, $2.00; berry bowl, $125.00+.

Beaded Block. Plates, $4.50 each; $8.00.
pitcher, $100.00; stemmed jelly,

Block Optic Block. Sugar bowl, footed tumbler, $5.00; salt shaker,
$3.00; plate, $7.00; ice tub, $15.00; $15.00.

Bowknot. Cup, $5.50; plate, $5.00; **sherbet, $6.50.**
berry bowl, $7.00; tumbler, $7.00;

Cherry Blossom. Cream and sugar, **$9.50; vegetable bowl, $13.00.**
$25.00; pitcher, $25.00; plate,

Chinex Classic. Cream and sugar, $2.00. $8.00; plate, $3.00; sherbet plate,

Circle. Goblet, $1.50; tumbler, $3.00; cup, $2.50; saucer, $1.00.

Colonial Block. Sugar bowl, $7.50.

Coronation. Berry bowl, $4.00; saucer, $4.50. large berry bowl, $9.00; cup and

Diana. Cream and sugar, $6.00;   plate, $3.00; cup and saucer, $5.00.

Floragold Louisa. Cream and sugar,   saucer, $7.50; candy dish, $25.00.
$7.00; pitcher, $17.50; cup and

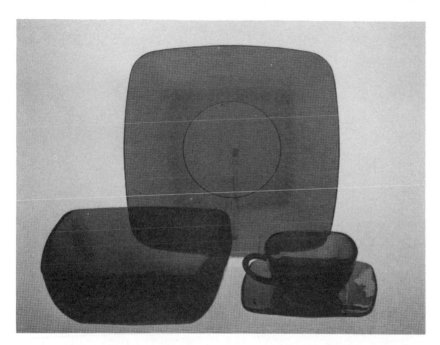

Forrest Green. Salad bowl, $5.00; plate, $2.50; cup and saucer, $3.00.

Hex Optic Honeycomb. Ice bucket, $3.50.
$7.50; salt shaker, $7.50; tumbler,

Lake Como. Cup and saucer, $3.00; plate, $3.00; salt and pepper, $15.00.

Mayfair Open Rose. Creamer, $9.50; cup and saucer, $21.00; can- dy dish, $26.00; cake plate, $20.00.

Moondrops. Cup and saucer, $9.00; salad plate, $4.00; small creamer, **$8.00; sugar bowl, $6.50.**

Mt. Pleasant Double Shield. Cup and saucer, $5.00; cream and sugar, **$14.00; plate, $6.00.**

Sierra, Pinwheel, bowl $5.00; plate $5.00-7.00; sugar & creamer $12.00.

Spiral. Plate $2.00; creamer $4.00;   sherbet $2.50.

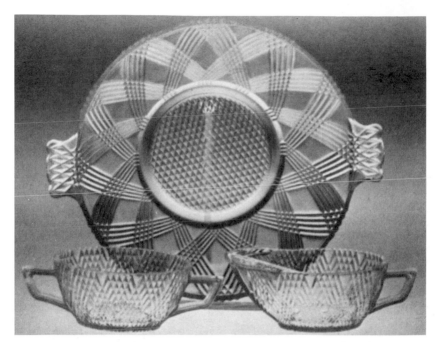

Starlight. Each piece worth $3.00-5.00.

$20.00; plates $5.00-7.00.

Sunflower. Tumbler $10.00; cup & $6.50.
saucer $7.50; plate $6.50; creamer

Swirl, Petal Swirl. Bowl $10.00; plate $5.00; salt $10.00; cup $3.00.

Tea Room. Cream & sugar set, $6.50.
$30.00; plate $18.00; small plate

Thistle, Bowl $75.00; cake plate $7.00.
$55.00; bowl $10.00; small plate

white and crystal. Most of the glassware can be found in pastel shades of translucent glass, and originally most was given away as premiums or sold at a very low price. Because so much of the glassware was produced, there are millions of pieces of Depression glass on the market and in private collections across the country. The collector should be very careful because reproduction Depression has been turning up around the country.

Disney Collectibles

Walt Disney created many characters that were immediately popular and manufacturers produced hundreds of different toys and likenesses of these. Mickey Mouse is by far the most popular, but Donald Duck, Snow White & the Seven Dwarfs, Pluto, Goofy, and many others follow close behind. Certain original Mickey Mouse watches bring $200.00-300.00 but there are several Mickey Mouse watches available some being produced today. The most popular Disney items are those from the 1930's and 1940's.

Figero Cat, cookie jar $50.00-60.00
Goofy, celluloid .... $100.00 +
Mickey Mouse doll, Stuffed, pie
  eyes, Steiff .... $500.00 +

Sharon Cabbage Rose. Sherbet, $6.50; salt shakers, $14.00 each; sugar bowl, $5.00; tumbler, $15.00; vegetable bowl, $7.00; plate, $7.00.

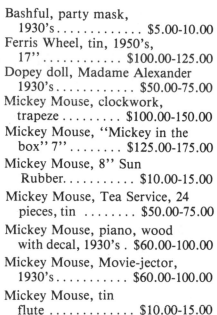

Bashful, party mask,
1930's $5.00-10.00
Ferris Wheel, tin, 1950's,
17" $100.00-125.00
Dopey doll, Madame Alexander
1930's $50.00-75.00
Mickey Mouse, clockwork,
trapeze $100.00-150.00
Mickey Mouse, "Mickey in the
box" 7" $125.00-175.00
Mickey Mouse, 8" Sun
Rubber. $10.00-15.00
Mickey Mouse, Tea Service, 24
pieces, tin $50.00-75.00
Mickey Mouse, piano, wood
with decal, 1930's . $60.00-100.00
Mickey Mouse, Movie-jector,
1930's $60.00-100.00
Mickey Mouse, tin
flute $10.00-15.00

Mickey Mouse banks, left: $100.00; right: $25.00.

The "Mickey Mouse Films" and "Mickey Mouse Cine Art Films" from the 1930's in original boxes are worth about $15.00-25.00 each. The Ingersol watch from the 1950's is unusual in that it has "Mickey Mouse" in script but no figure. The ceramic figure is from the early 1960's and accompanied a watch.

105

♪ WHO'S AF'AID OF THE
BIG BAD WOLF? ♪

BEST WISHES TO HAROLD FRANKLIN,
FROM — WALT DISNEY —

A watercolor of The Three Pigs from Walt Disney Studio is worth about $400.00 +.

Minnie Mouse, mask,
   1930's $7.50-11.50
Minnie Mouse, roly poly,
   celluloid $2.00-3.00
Peter Pan, marionette,
   1950's $7.00-10.00
Pinocchio, hand puppet $2.00-3.50
Pluto, wood, 1930's .. $18.00-25.00
Sleepy, mask, 1930's ... $5.00-7.50
Sleepy, 5" rubber figure,
   1930's $10.00-20.00
Snow White and 7 Dwarfs,
   musical top $15.00-20.00
3 little pigs, wood pig,
   1930's $18.00-25.00
Zorro ring $4.50-6.75
Cinderella wrist watch $25.00-30.00
Mickey Mouse, fireman
   mug $10.00-12.00
Mickey Mouse, teaspoon,
   silverplate $5.00-8.00
Pinocchio, wooden doll,
   11" $50.00-65.00
Mickey Mouse, target, round,
   1930's $20.00-30.00
Minnie Mouse, wood doll,
   3½" $45.00-50.00

Disney books from the 1930's. "The Adventures of Mickey Mouse" $50.00; Peculiar Penguins $15.00-25.00.

Minnie Mouse, cookie
   cutter $10.00-12.00
Donald Duck, pencil
   sharpener $2.50-3.50
Fantasia Movie program,
   1940's $7.00-10.00

Dollhouses

The increased interest in dolls and all types of miniatures has lead to a renewed popularity of dollhouses. All types are collectible, from the folding paper dollhouse books, to

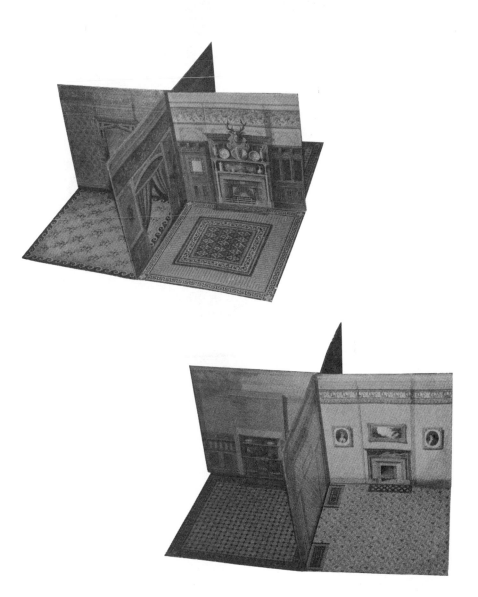

A folding paper dollhouse made by   McLoughlin.

This lithographed and wood dollhouse was probably made by Bliss. Bliss dollhouses were extremely popular during the late 19th Century.

the elaborate wood replicas, and anything in between. Quality and authenticity are generally the value determining factors and some dollhouses are worth thousands of dollars. Usually any wood dollhouse of good construction and true scale will run a minimum of $200.00-300.00.

Dolls Antique

Antique dolls, produced from 1850 to the mid 1930's have reached a new high in popularity. Some ex-amples bring hundreds, even thousands of dollars. Dolls produced by Armand Marseille, Schoenhut, Kestner, Simon & Halbig and other major manufacturers usually bring premium prices. Prices here are for dolls in excellent condition and completely restored. Beware of new dolls that are made to resemble antique dolls.

Alt, Beck & Gottschalk, 13'',
   open mouth .... $150.00 +

Amberg, "Vanta Baby", 24",
  1920's, ... $75.00-100.00
Amuso, 13" Oriental . . . $400.00 +
Arnold, 15½", 1880's . . $200.00 +
Averill, Baby Hendren . . $125.00 +
Bahr & Proschild, 10",
  toddler . . . . $350.00 +
Bru, 19" Bebe Teteur,
  1870's . . . . $2000.00 +
Buschow & Beck, tin head,
  Minerva $90.00-125.00
Cameo, Kewpie, cloth body,
  composition head $110.00-130.00
Denamur, 14" socket head, closed
  mouth $900.00
Effanbee, 11", Patsy Jr.,
  composition, 1930 . $50.00-75.00

This antique papier mache clown is worth $170.00 or more.

Fulpher, 15",
  composition . . . . $300.00 +
Ernst Heubach, 19½",
  baby . . . . $200.00 +
Kammer & Reinhardt, Mein
  Liebling, 23" . . . . $1500.00 +
Kley & Hahn, 23", socket head,
  1902 . . . . $300.00 +
A. Lanternier & Cie, Laughing
  Limoge, 14" $100.00-125.00
Morimura Brothers, 11",
  baby $100.00-115.00
Parson Jackson, 10" Biskoline baby
  1910 . . . . $175.00-200.00
Putnam, Bye-Lo Baby,
  16" . . . . $450.00 +
Herman Steiner, 13" socket head,
  boy . . . . $150.00 +

Antique papier mache doll from Germany, $65.00.

109

Jules Steiner, Bebe Parisien,
14" . . . . $1000.00 +

Ferte, 15" composition & wood,
1870's . . . . $1000.00 +

Gebruder Heubach, papier mache,
socket head, 8" . . . . . . $600.00 +

Adolf Wislizenus, 23" socket
head . . . . $250.00 +

Jackie Coogan, Japanese,
bisque $35.00-40.00

This 20" Alfred E. Newman doll,
Mad Magazine's "Cover Boy"
from the early 1960's is worth about
$60.00-70.00.

A 17" blonde china doll, $200.00.

Dolls, Modern

Modern dolls, those produced from
the 1930's to present, are extremely
popular flea market items. These
modern dolls have contributed
greatly to the overall appeal of the
doll collecting hobby. Dolls not currently in production or discontinued
variations of current dolls are most
collectible. Character dolls,
especially those of the 1930's and
1940's are much in demand.

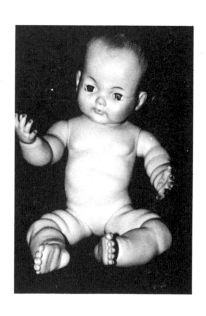

This 12" Bye Bye Baby is from
about 1964. It can be found for
$2.00-5.00.

Nancy Ann, "Debbie",
   10½" $5.00-10.00

Truly Scrumptious,
   1960's $10.00-15.00

Patootie, 16", 1965 . . . . $4.00-5.00

Baby bundles, 14",
   1960's $1.00-2.00

Marigold, 19", 1960's . . $5.00-7.00

Cuddly Baby, 1960's . . . $1.00-2.00

Pri-thilla, 1950's $10.00-12.00

Monica Joan, 11" . . . $60.00-70.00

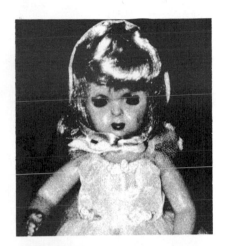

Tiny Terri Lee in a ballerina outfit, from the late 1950's, is valued at $25.00-$35.00.

Mortimer Snerd from the 1960's, $30.00.

Captain Kangaroo, 1967,
   Mattel $5.00-7.00
Nancy Nonsense, 18"
   1970's $15.00-20.00
Tina, 18", 1950's $8.00-10.00
Lovely Liz, 1960's,
   15" $8.00-12.00
Nun, 16", 1930's $40.00-50.00
Betty, 16" 1960's $6.00-8.00
Cindy Lou, 12", 1950's . $3.00-5.00

Ferrandiz

Ferrandiz figures are wood carved art from the Anri Company based on the paintings of Juan Ferrandiz Castells of Barcellona, Spain. These high quality art pieces are of recent manufacture, but still carry relatively high prices.

Romeo, 6" $185.00-200.00
Sharing, 3" $45.00-55.00
Weary Traveler, 3" . . $50.00-55.00
Night, Night, 3" $45.00-60.00
Native Girl, 6" $100.00-150.00
Love Gift, 6" $90.00-110.00
Journey, 3" $75.00-90.00
Joseph, 6" $110.00-115.00
Infant, (Jesus), 2" . . . $70.00-75.00
The Helper, 5" $125.00-135.00
Have You Heard?,
   6" $125.00-150.00
The Good Shepard,
   3" $45.00-55.00
Girl With Rooster . . . $90.00-105.00
Friendship, 3" $55.00-90.00
A Free Ride, 6" $80.00-90.00

This 6'' Flower Girl Ferrandiz figure can be found for $200.00

Fiesta

Fiesta is a brightly colored, heavy ironstone dinnerware produced by the Homer Laughlin Co. from 1936 until 1971. The lines and styles of this popular collectible are right out of the Art Deco period. Fiesta pieces are easily recognized because of their bright, gay colors, smooth graceful lines and distinctive pattern shapes. Originally Fiesta was produced in red, dark blue, old ivory, yellow, light green, and turquois. Though there were other colors produced, anything but these are of later manufacture. Harlequin & Riviera, similar but less expensive lines of dinnerware were also produced by Homer Laughlin Co.

Dinner plate, 10"	$3.00-5.00
Compartment plate, 11"	$9.50-12.00
Salad bowl, small	$10.00-15.00
Dessert bowl, 6"	$7.50-10.00
Tea cup	$7.00-10.00
Saucer	$1.00-3.00
Disc water pitcher, 2 quart	$18.00-20.00
Tumbler	$12.00-15.00
Covered sugar bowl	$7.50-10.00
Salt & pepper	$8.00-12.00
Oval platter, 12"	$8.00-12.00
Fruit bowl, 11"	$35.00-40.00
Vase, 12"	$75.00-100.00
Tea pot large	$25.00-30.00
Chop plate, handled, 13"	$32.00-37.00
Juice pitcher, 30 oz.	$7.50--10.00

Two popular Fiesta pieces, both dropped from the line in the 1940's. The odd shaped carafe on the left was produced in six colors and because of its styling is a favorite with collectors. It is valued at about $30.00-35.00. The ice pitcher on the right, also made in six colors is worth about $25.00-30.00.

Fiesta plates and bowls, $2.00-4.50.

Top; nested bowl set; bottom: about $15.00-25.00.
childrens set. Each piece is worth

This juice set, pitcher and 6 tumblers is valued at $75.00-100.00.

Juice pitcher, 30 oz.
   red $25.00-30.00
Ash tray $15.00-20.00
Syrup pitcher $55.00-65.00
Bread & butter $2.50-3.50
Coffee pot $27.50-30.00
Casserole $25.00-30.00
Creamer, 4" $25.00-30.00
Oval platter, 12½" .. $22.50-27.00

Fire Fighting Collectibles

Anything related to fighting and detecting fires is considered collectible. Personal items used by firemen, station house equipment, fire fighting equipment, home extinguishers, parade uniforms, etc., are all subjects of search by enthusiasts of fire fighting. Early items, such as leather helmets and buckets are especially desirable. Also equipment made from brass, copper, gold and silver demands a high price.

Fireman's trumpet, brass octagonal, 1880's $150.00
Alarm bell, brass gong on walnut $165.00-180.00
Postcard, Horse drawn fire engine $3.00-5.00
Postcard, Horse drawn engine in action $5.00-7.00
Postcard, group of firemen in front of station, pre-1920............ $3.00-4.00
Fire mark, painted tree, cast iron $100.00-115.00
Brass fire nozzle, 12" Eureka $50.00-60.00
Uniform shirt, flap front, red wool $60.00-65.00
Toy cast iron pump wagon and team, 18" .... $250.00 +
Pinback button, Steelton PA, fireman's face $5.00-6.00
Brass fire nozzle, 20" $100.00-120.00
Ax, painted handle, spike on one end $25.00-30.00

Leather fire bucket with original paint and handle. This is an excellent example and worth about $250.00 or more.

Leather bucket, 13" high,
  no handle $125.00
Fire extinguisher, brass and copper
  24" cylinder $35.00-40.00
Fire alarm box, iron, gabled
  top, red $165.00-180.00
Glass fire grenades in metal
  holder $15.00-20.00
Lantern, Dietz, red globe . . . $50.00
Helmet with Eagle, leather,
  1800's . . , ... $100.00

Fireplace Accessories

For many years, fireplaces have served as sources of heat, for cooking, and as a place of decoration and luxury. Equipment has been made in a number of materials to differing degrees of beauty for both the decoration of a fireplace as well as the practical use. Most pieces of accessories are collected for the purpose they were created--to enhance the beauty and serviceability of the fireplace.

Bellows, 19" $30.00-50.00
Fireplace oven, tin, covered
  cylindrical $130.00-140.00
Fireplace oven, open
  style $60.00-70.00
Hearth broom,
  splintered $100.00-115.00
Trammel, racket
  type $40.00-50.00
Heating trivet, 3 legs . . . . $125.00 +
Frying pan, extra long handle,
  iron $135.00-145.00
Peel, long handle,
  iron $80.00-90.00
Coal saver, wire basket with
  pole $10.00-15.00
Andirons, cast iron,
  plain . . . . $50.00-75.00 pr.
Popcorn popper, wrought
  iron $30.00-35.00
Andirons, cast iron,
  figural $35.00-45.00
Andirons, brass . . . $150.00-175.00
Hearth broiler, wrought
  iron $175.00-200.00
Spit stand, tripod,
  iron $125.00-150.00
Ember tongs, wrought iron, ball
  knob $25.00-30.00
Fender, brass, 54",
  1800's $175.00-200.00
Coal hod, wood and
  brass $100.00-125.00
Poker, tongs, shovel, holder,
  brass $90.00-115.00
Firescreen,
  needlepoint $150.00-225.00
Andirons, brass, claw
  feet . . . . $250.00 +

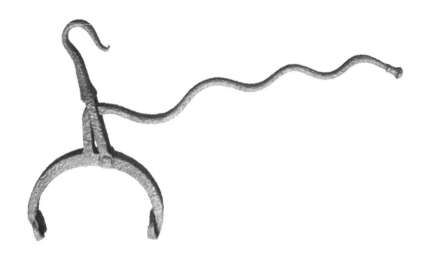

This kettle tilter is made of cast iron and is from the late 1700's or early 1800's, $225.00 + .

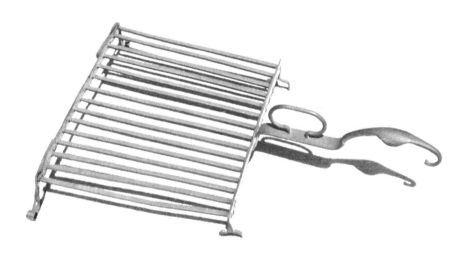

This early 19th century gridiron was used to broil meat or fish in the fireplace and can be found for $175.00 or more.

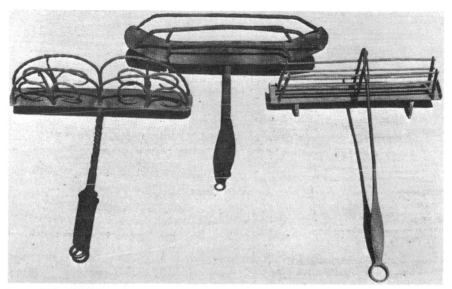

Iron fireplace toasters used in the late 1700's. The fancy example at left could bring as much as $200.00. The plain ones, $100.00.

Flow Blue

Flow Blue is an English china. During the firing, the blue appears to have run from the design giving the china a smeared look. Pieces of Flow Blue were made in many patterns in the 1800's by several different potteries. Collectors are paying high prices for good quality Flow Blue today. The following listings include pattern names.

Cereal bowl, Oregon . $27.50-35.00

Covered sugar bowl,
    Shanghai $100.00-125.00

Chop plate, LaBelle .. $70.00-85.00

Milk pitcher, Hindustan . $150.00+

Sauce dish, Marie $12.00-15.00

Creamer, Waldorf ... $55.00-75.00

Dresser tray, Waldorf $50.00-60.00

Covered cheese dish, Kiji $125.00+

Handled cake plate,
    Watteau $50.00-60.00

Honey dish, Chapoo . $25.00-30.00

Bone dish, Celtic $18.00-25.00

Sauceboat, Oriental .. $70.00-85.00

Serving bowl,
    Normandy $30.00-45.00

Chocolate pot,
    Warwick $90.00-100.00

Vase, Azalea .... $300.00+

Fruit Bowl,
    Melbourne $90.00-115.00

Soup plate, Manilla,
    10½" $62.00-75.00

Teapot, Hong Kong .... $125.00+

Covered vegetable dish,
    Lugano $75.00-80.00

Relish tray, Blue
    Danube $30.00-40.00

Platter, Argyle, 12" .. $55.00-70.00

Gravy boat,
    Devonwood $25.00-30.00

Wash basin, Iris ...... $175.00+

Cup & saucer,
    Arcadia $35.00-50.00

Typical Flow Blue plate. Note how the color seems to have been smeared past the outer edges of the pattern. This would be valued at about $25.00 or more.

Fountain Pens

Only recently have collectors been grabbing up all of those beautiful old fountain pens that were so commonplace in the 1920's, 30's and 40's. The most popular are the name brands and the most valuable are the gold pens. Many sets of fountain pens with matching pencils can be found and since this hobby is still relatively new, prices are fairly reasonable for quality items. Prices here are for pens in excellent condition and in working order. The alert collector should also be on the lookout for damaged or worn pens to be

PLATE II WATERMAN 1920-1926

Waterman pens from 1920 to 1926. A. Model 52, $25.00-35.00; B. Desk Ripple, $10.00-12.00; C. 54 Ripple, $20.00-30.00; D. 58 Ripple, $100.00 +; E. 5 Ripple, $20.00-30.00; F. Pencil Ripple, $7.50-10.00; G. 7 Ripple, $30.00-35.00; H. Same as D.

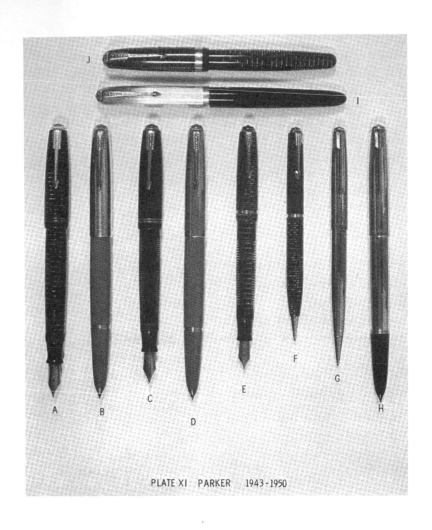

PLATE XI PARKER 1943-1950

Parkers pens from the 1940's $5.00-10.00 each except the "51" at right, $15.00-20.00.

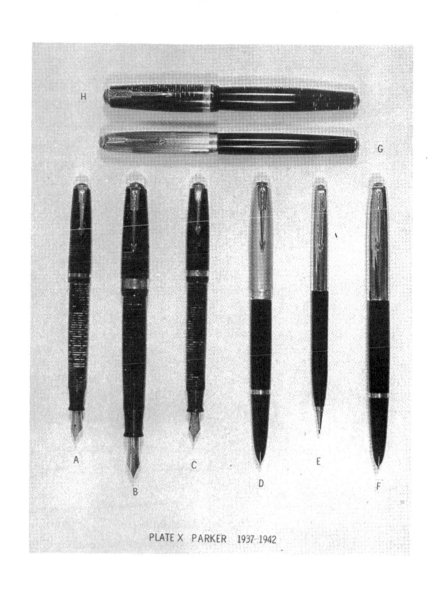

PLATE X PARKER 1937-1942

Parkers pens from the 1930's, $15.00-30.00.

1923 Parker Duofolds, $110.00 each.

used as parts in repairing similar pens.

Waterman

Lady Patricia, 1928 .. $12.00-15.00
Patrician, 1928 ...... $65.00-75.00
Model 7, 1930 .... $25.00-30.00
Model 94, 1932 ...... $10.00-12.00
Lady Patricia, 1936 .. $15.00-20.00
Ideal Ink View, 1942 . $10.00-12.00
Commando, 1943 ..... $8.00-10.00
100 Year Pen, 1944 ... $10.00-12.00
100 Year Pen, 1945 ... $12.00-15.00
Citation, 1946 .... $7.00-10.00

Parker

6 Lucky Curve, 1894 . $40.00-50.00
37 Lucky Curve, 1895 $20.00-30.00
Lucky Curve, 1917, push
    button $20.00-30.00
Lucky Curve, 1917 ... $75.00-80.00
Duofold Senior, Big Red,
    1921 .... $120.00 +
Duofold Jr., 1923 .... $15.00-20.00
Lady Duofold, 1923 .. $20.00-30.00
Duofold Senior, Canada $120.00 +

Wahl-Eversharp

Gold Seal Eversharp,
    1930 .... $15.00-20.00
Doric Ladies' Gold Seal,
    1931 .... $15.00-20.00
Midget $10.00-12.00
Silver Seal Doric $12.00-15.00
Skyline Pen, 1941 ...... $4.00-5.00
Fifth Avenue, 1944 ... $12.00-15.00

Sheaffer

White Dot Lifetime,
    1922 .... $35.00-45.00
Ladies White Dot Lifetime,
    1941 .... $8.00-12.00
Crest White Dot Lifetime,
    1940 .... $35.00-45.00
Crest Pencil, 1940 .... $15.00-20.00
Vigilant White Dot,
    1941 .... $5.00-10.00
Triumph Lifetime,
    1942 .... $25.00-35.00

French Dolls

Antique dolls produced in France have become very popular and valuable in this country. The original beauty and craftsmanship are still evident in these dolls and for well represented examples in original dress, prices soar. Bru dolls seem to be especially desirable.

Unis, 12", 5 piece
    body $150.00-250.00
Jules Steiner, 29" ..... $1500.00 +
Schoneau and Hoffmeister,
    Hanna $200.00-300.00
S.F.J.B., 18", mechanical
    walker $500.00-700.00
Schmitt & Fils, 23" ..... $700.00 +
Rabery & Delphieu, 17" $1000.00 +
Jumeau, 16", 1906 . $450.00-600.00
Danel & Cie, 21½",
    Paris Bebe .... $1000.00 +
Fleischmann & Blodel, 20½"
    Eden Bebe .... $700.00 +
Jumeau, 15",
    Bebe Jumeau .... $600.00 +

This French S.F.B.J. in original costume is worth $2,500.00+ in ex- cellent condition.

27'' Bru, composition and wood. $5000.00.
This rare example is worth

21½" Danel & Cie Paris Bebe   valued at $1300.00 or more.

Fruit Jars

Fruit jars are glass jars that can be sealed from the outside air and are used in preserving fruits and vegetables. Through the years, the jars have had very few changes. The enclosures, on the other hand, have had a gradual evolution from clamps, bails, glass lids and other complicated devices to today's easy-to-use models. Fruit jars are available in many sizes and colors and have been manufactured by a multitude of companies. Prices here are for jars with the original enclosures, and no cracks or chips. Factory flaws are sometimes desirable if the flaw is a rare type.

A&C, 1885, glass lid and wire clip, aqua $50.00-75.00

Acme, 1920's, glass lid, wire bail, clear $3.00-8.00

Advance, 1885, glass lid, metal clamp $30.00-75.00

Agee Queen, 1925, glass lid $5.00-10.00

Anderson Preserving Co., 1920's, metal lid $3.00-6.00

Atlas H A Mason #2, 1920, metal screw band $2.00-5.00

Ball Deluxe Jar, 1930, glass lid $4.00-8.00

Ball Special Wide Mouth, 1910-1915, zinc lid . . . $1.00-2.00

Bennetts #1, 1900, screw top $75.00-100.00

The Best, 1875, glass stopper $10.00-18.00

Bosco Double Seal, 1920, glass lid $4.00-8.00

Canadian Sure Seal, 1920-1940, metal screw band $2.00-4.00

Cassidy, 1885, glass lid, wire bail $75.00-150.00

Chef, 1908, glass lid, wire bail $4.00-8.00

Clark's Peerless, 1882, glass lid, wire bail $10.00-20.00

Corona Jar, 1925, zinc lid $2.00-4.00

Crown #2, 1870-1890, glass lid, metal screw band . . . $6.00-10.00

Cunningham & Ihmsen, 1868-1879, wax sealer $20.00-30.00

Curtis & Moore, 1900, glass lid, wire bail $25.00-35.00

Decker's Victor, 1935, glass lid, wire bail $25.00-35.00

Dominion Mason, 1915-1920, zinc lid $2.00-4.00

The Eclipse, 1865-1875, wax sealer $65.00-85.00

Federal Fruit Jar, 1895, glass lid, wire bail $15.00-30.00

The Gayner, 1915-1925, glass lid, wire bail $9.00-15.00

Fruit Jars. Queen Improved Shield, $10.00-20.00; Schram Automatic Sealer, 1909, $6.00-12.00; Swayzee's Improved Mason, $4.00-8.00.

Fruit Jars. Gem Improved, $10.00-20.00; Kinsells True Mason, $6.00-12.00; The Mason, $4.00-6.00; Presto Glass Top, $2.00-4.00.

Gem Improved, 1860's,
   zinc band $10.00-20.00
Harris Improved, 1875-1880,
   glass lid, iron clamp $50.00-75.00
The Ideal, 1895-1900,
   zinc lid $10.00-25.00
Jewel Jar #1, 1915-1920, zinc
   screw band $4.00-8.00
The Kalamazoo, 1870-1875,
   wax sealer $8.00-12.00
Lafayette #1, 1864,
   wax dipped cork . $175.00-250.00
Michigan Mason, 1911-1916,
   zinc lid $5.00-10.00
National, 1885,
   metal lid $35.00-60.00
O.G., 1900, glass lid,
   wire bail $15.00-20.00
The Pearl, 1860's,
   screw band $10.00-20.00
Perfect Seal, 1925 ...... $4.00-8.00
Pine Mason, 1927-1929,
   zinc lid $4.00-8.00
Presto Supreme Mason,
   1930's $1.00-2.00
Royal, 1900, glass lid,
   wire bail $10.00-25.00
Sanford, 1900, metal
   screw band $10.00-15.00
Sanitary, 1900,
   glass lid $10.00-15.00
Tight Seal, 1908,
   glass lid $2.00-4.00

Gambling Devices

Gambling, games of chance, cheating devices, machines and pieces from games are all collectible. Slot machines, once common in many public places prior to the Depression are in great demand as are "layouts" or surfaces designed for gambling games. Cheating devices, because of their rarity, usually command a large price tag.

A dice cage. This plated model is worth about $150.00-250.00.

A 16" roulette wheel worth $225.00 or more.

Prices for gambling machines are for those in excellent working condition.

Slot machine, Mills HiTop, 1930's .... $750.00+

Slot machine, Mills Black Cherry, 1930's .... $750.00+

Ivory dice cup, carved, late 1800's $125.00-200.00

Dice cups, leather or wood, late 1800's $25.00-50.00

Corner rounder for playing cards, late 1800's $500.00-700.00

Shear trimmer for playing cards, late 1800's .... $750.00+

Card press, wood, 1800's $300.00+

Hazard horn for dice, wood, 1800's $175.00-200.00

Slot machine, Dutch Boy $600.00+

Layout for "Chuck-a-Luck", H.C. Evans, wood trim .... $500.00+

Slot machine, Mills Black Beauty .... $750.00+

Keno Goose, wood with ivory number balls, 1800's . $500.00-750.00

Poker chips, ivory, 1800's ...... each $10.00-15.00

Slot machine, Fey Silver Dollar, late 1920's .... $800.00+

Roulette chips, ivory, multicolored, early 1900's .. each $10.00-15.00

Roulette wheel, wood and chrome, 16" diameter, late 1800's $225.00-325.00

Roulette wheel, wood and chrome, 24" diameter, late 1800's .... $750.00+

Guillotine trimmer for playing cards, brass .... $1000.00+

Poker cards, Steamboat deck, late 1800's $35.00-40.00

Bingo cage, wire on wood base, 1920's or 1930's ... $60.00-65.00

Dice cage, brass, 1920's $175.00-200.00

Roulette wheel, traveling, in oak case $200.00-250.00

Punch board, Coca-Cola, girl & pool table, 1920's .... $250.00+

Punch board, Coca-Cola, cartoon man on hot day, 1920's .... $250.00+

Slot machine, Mills Jockey .... $1800.00+

Slot machine, Mills Bursting Cherry .... $1200.00+

Slot machine, Mills Roman Head .... $1500.00+

The "Bug" holdout. This cheating device, an ivory button is valued at $125.00-175.00.

Games

Game collecting probably began as an offshoot of the popular hobby of toy collecting, but has grown to be a well regarded hobby in its own right. Many games produced around the turn of the century or before are still being played today with little or no changes. Prices here are for games in good condition and in original boxes with no missing pieces.

Table croquet, wood, wood case,
    early 1900's $15.00-25.00
Centennalia, 1870's . . $55.00-65.00
Lindy, 1920's $20.00-25.00
Touring, 1920's $10.00-15.00
Uncle Wiggily, pin-up $15.00-20.00

African Hunter, darts,
    1930's $25.00-30.00
Authors, 1890's $12.00-15.00
Barney Google and Sparkplug,
    1920's $50.00-60.00
Lotto, 1890's $20.00-25.00
Old Maid, McLoughlin
    Brothers $5.00-7.00
Rook, 1915-1920 . . . . . . $5.00-7.00
Snap $12.00-15.00
Seige, early 1900's . . . $25.00-30.00
Battle of Tanks, 1940 . . . $5.00-7.50
Billy Whiskers $17.50-22.50
Blondie & Dagwood,
    1940's $10.00-15.00
Fish Pond, 1890's $15.00-17.00
Battaan, 1940's $5.00-7.00
Lone Star Dominoes . . $7.50-12.00

Two primitive checker boards of wood. Walnut shells or dried corn slices were sometimes used as checkers. The small board is worth $18.00-25.00, the large one will bring $60.00-80.00.

A 7½" American Indian baby made by Heubach - Kopplesdorf, $250.00-300.00.

German Dolls

German dolls are especially appealing to doll collectors. Best known for the children and lifelike babies, these dolls are relatively expensive when in original clothes and in good condition. Also see Armand Marseille, Kestern and Simon & Halbig.

4" bisque, painted features,
    toddler $50.00-100.00
Herm Steiner, baby,
    16" $250.00-300.00
Schoenau & Hoffmeister,
    22" child $300.00-400.00
Bruno Schmidt, 12"
    child $100.00-150.00
Reinecke, 15" baby $200.00-250.00

This Kammer-Rhinehart 11'' boy is worth about $1200.00.

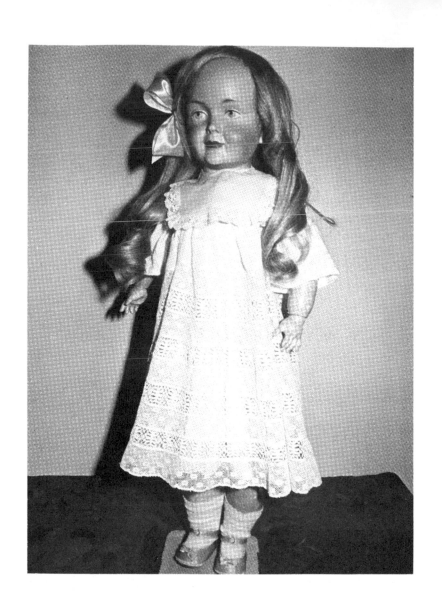

Kley & Hahn 24'' girl, $1200.00.

Limbach, bisque
    baby $200.00-250.00
Kley & Hahn, 14" girl . . $700.00 +
Kammer & Rinehart,
    14" baby $200.00-250.00
Heubach - Koppelsdorf, 9" black
    baby, grass skirt . . . . . $350.00 +
Otto Gans, 20"
    baby $200.00-250.00

Glass Candlesticks

Nearly all of the glass houses in this country produced candlesticks. The many patterns, varieties and styles of the candlesticks produced through the years offer the collector a limitless source for collecting. Naturally, the more popular glass companies are the makers of the more popular candlesticks. More collectors are specializing in candlesticks and as the popularity increases, the value is also increasing.

Tiffin, translucent green,
    2" square base $8.00-10.00
Boston & Sandwich, crucifix,
    11", milkglass . . . . . . $500 + pair

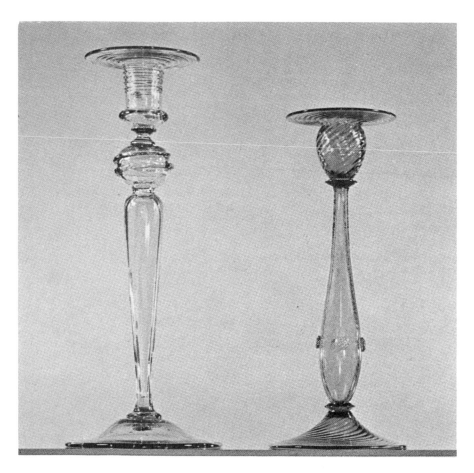

Two candlesticks from the Steuben Glass Co., Corning New York, each is worth $130.00-170.00.

Boston & Sandwich, dolphin, white,
    blue socket . . . . $200.00 +
Butler Bros., Golden Assortment,
    7" . . . . $30.00-35.00 pair
Butler Bros., Handled Colonial,
    clear, 4½" $8.00-10.00
Cambridge, shell with prism,
    7" . . . . $35.00-40.00 pair
Cambridge, twist, pastel green,
    8½" . . . . $40.00-45.00 pair
Central Ribbed, amber,
    console set $50.00-60.00
Clarke, Hobstar,
    8½" . . . . $50.00-55.00 pair
Fenton, Horn-of-Plenty, 5½",
    3 piece set $35.00-40.00
Fostoria, Orleans,
    2" $10.00-12.00
Heisey, Flute with Handle,
    7¼" $50.00-60.00
Heisey, Ribbed, 9¼" $40.00-50.00
Heisey, Colonial,
    6¼" . . . . $65.00-70.00 pair
Imperial, Newbound,
    4½" . . . . $25.00-30.00 pair
Indiana, Garland,
    5½" $15.00-20.00
Jeannette, Iris, iridescent,
    5½" $10.00-12.00
McKee, Vulcan, 6" . . $14.00-16.00
Rosenthal, Tulips,
    15½" . . . . $200.00 + pair
Westmoreland, Lotus,
    3¾" $12.00-15.00

Goofus Glass

Goofus Glass was first produced in this country around the turn of the century and continued to be manufactured until shortly after World War I. Originally, it was given away as prizes at carnivals and fairs. Goofus is clear glass that has been embossed with designs and then painted bright, flashy colors, usually red and gold. The most popular motifs are roses, flowers, berries or animals. Most pieces found today are beginning to peel.

Prices here are for pieces in good condition with original paint.

Dinner plate, roses, red and
    gold $12.00-15.00
Salad bowl, roses, red and
    gold $12.00-15.00
Pickle jar, grapes, purple and
    black $8.00-12.00
Dinner plate, grapes, red and
    gold $12.00-17.00
Bowl, large, carnations, red and
    gold $17.00-22.00
Cake plate, grapes, red and
    silver $15.00-20.00
Salad plate, strawberries, red and
    gold $10.00-12.00

Blue and gold Goofus is not as plentiful as red and gold. A 12″ tall vase with daisies is valued at about $15.00.

137

This large Goofus glass plate is worth about $12.00-15.00.

Salad bowl, grapes, purple and
    gold $15.00-20.00

Relish dish, floral, red, green,
    and gold $15.00-18.00

Small nut bowl, floral, red
    and gold $10.00-15.00

Dinner plate, carnations, red and
    gold $8.00-12.00

Powder jar, roses, red and
    gold $17.00-25.00

Bowl, large, chrysanthemums, red
    and gold $15.00-20.00

Graniteware

Graniteware or enameled ware is the name given to enameled tinware. It was first manufactured in the United States in the 1870's, and was immediately popular. The majority of pieces have either a marbelized, shaded or spattered look and were produced in a variety of colors. Prices here are for pieces in good condition with minimal chips and no dents, holes or discoloration. Green, brown, or purple enameled ware are somewhat more valuable than the blue or gray pieces.

Graniteware cooking aids. The funnels at the top are worth $5.00-10.00; pudding molds in the center, $5.00-10.00; cake pan, center right, $12.00-15.00; corn bread pan, $3.00-6.00.

Graniteware. The white and black frying pans are worth about $6.00-12.00; the spoons and spatula, $3.00-7.00; the shallow baking pan at bottom, $8.00-12.00.

Granite dinnerware. Mugs and cups can be found for $2.00-5.00 each; plates for $6.00-12.00. The white plate is only worth $2.00-3.00.

Guns, Antique

Guns manufactured before 1898 are considered antique firearms. Prices have been climbing steadily on guns in the past few years but the collectors are not buying the guns to shoot, but to fill collections. Many of the old guns will not stand up to today's powder. Beware of reproductions and imitations in this area because many commemoratives, reissues and look-alikes are on the market today. Prices here are for completely original firearms, in excellent condition with no flaws or damage.

Allen & Wheelock, 44 revolver,
   percussion, 1850's .... $300.00 +
Colt Patterson, 28 revolver,
   percussion .... $2000.00 +
Colt 1851 Navy, revolver,
   percussion .... $750.00 +
Colt 1849 Pocket, revolver,
   conversion .... $200.00 +
Manhattan Navy, 36 revolver,
   percussion .... $1500.00 +
Pecare & Smith,
   pepperbox .... $900.00 +

Starr, 44 revolver,
   percussion .... $300.00 +
Tryon derringer, 41
   percussion .... $275.00 +
Union Arms, pepperbox $200.00 +
Remington-Beals, 1860, Navy,
   percussion .... $325.00 +
Remington Frontier, 44-40
   cartridge .... $400.00 +
Smith & Wesson #1, Issue #1,
   cartridge .... $350.00 +
Smith & Wesson Schofield,
   cartridge .... $600.00 +
Whitney Beals, ring trigger,
   percussion .... $200.00 +
Slotter & Co., derringer . $300.00 +
Metropolitian, 36 revolver,
   percussion .... $225.00 +
Hawes & Waggoner,
   derringer .... $400.00 +
Hopkins & Allen, 31 revolver,
   percussion $150.00-200.00
Winchester Henry Rifle $2500.00 +
Winchester Model 1873
   rifle .... $300.00 +
Allen & Wheelock revolving
   rifle .... $750.00 +
Cochran revolving rifle $1500.00 +
Warner Pocket, 28 revolver,
   percussion .... $200.00 +

A Spencer percussion rifle from the 1860's, **$750.00 +** .

Smith & Wesson Model 17 K-22 Masterpiece, $145.00-180.00; and

Ruger Mark I Target, $80.00-110.00.

Guns, Modern

Modern guns are becoming more and more popular even though legislators are enacting stricter gun laws. The buyer should be aware of the legislation in his state before purchasing firearms and the seller should also know the procedures and limitations under the law. Prices here are for guns (used) in excellent condition with no flaws.

Handguns

Astra 1911, semi-
  automatic $75.00-85.00
Bauer Stainless, semi-
  automatic $75.00-90.00
Bayard 1980, semi-
  automatic $100.00-120.00
Beretta 71, semi-
  automatic $110.00-135.00
Browning 1910, semi-
  automatic $155.00-190.00

Charter Arms Bulldog,
  revolver $100.00-125.00
Colt 1911, semi-
  automatic $255.00-325.00
Colt 1911A1 Military, semi-
  automatic $230.00-275.00
Colt Police Positive,
  revolver $170.00-190.00
Dan Wesson II,
  revolver $100.00-125.00
Harrington & Richardson 40,
  revolver $100.00-120.00
High Standard HDM, semi-
  automatic $185.00-225.00
Iver Johnson 57,
  revolver $60.00-70.00
Llama Comanche,
  revolver $160.00-200.00
Remington, derringer ... $300.00+
Ruger Blackhawk 30,
  revolver $140.00-175.00
Sauer 1913, semi-
  automatic $120.00-150.00
Smith & Wesson Victory,
  revolver $145.00-180.00

143

Smith & Wesson 17,
K-22 .... $145.00-180.00
Smith & Wesson 10 . $90.00-115.00
Star Model A, semi-
automatic $150.00-180.00
Walther PPK, semi-
automatic .... $280.00 +
Welbey & Scott Mark I,
semi-automatic ...... $225.00 +

Shotguns

Armalite AR-17,
semi-automatic ...... $500.00 +
AYA Matador, double
barrel .... $250.00 +
Baikal MC 21,
semi-automatic ...... $200.00 +
Baker Black Beauty
Special .... $425.00 +
Beretta 409 PB double
barrel .... $350.00 +
Harrington & Richardson 158,
single shot $50.00-60.00
High Standard Flite King Special
pump $145.00-180.00
Ithaca 37V $175.00-215.00
Kessler, 3 shot $65.00-75.00
L.C. Smith, double
barrel .... $500.00 +
Marlin 28, pump .... $275.00 +
Mossberg 83D, bolt
action $50.00-60.00
Noble 40, pump ... $100.00-120.00
Parker Trojan, double
barrel .... $500.00 +

Premier Continental, double
barrel $190.00-225.00
Remington 1100,
semi-automatic ...... $200.00 +
Remington 870,
pump $160.00-190.00
Richland 202, double
barrel .... $250.00 +
Sauer Royal, double
barrel .... $500.00 +
Savage 720,
semi-automatic .. $145.00-180.00
Stevens, 180, single
shot $75.00-90.00
Universal 101, single
shot $50.00-60.00
Weatherby Regency, double
barrel .... $600.00 +
Winchester Model 97,
pump .... $300.00 +
Winchester Model 37, single
shot $75.00-95.00

Rifles

Anschutz 141, bolt
action $150.00-190.00
BSA 12, single
shot $160.00-200.00
Browning BL-22, lever
action $115.00-145.00
Harrington & Richardson 765, bolt
action $30.00-40.00
High Standard Hi Power, bolt
action $195.00-240.00
Ithaca 49, lever action $30.00-40.00

Fox Model B double barrel shotgun.

Winchester Model 70 rifle.

Ruger Model 77 Magnum rifle.

Marlin 36A, lever
action $160.00-200.00

Marlin 39A, lever
action $120.00-135.00

Mauser 660, bolt
action $325.00-350.00

Mossberg 42B, bolt
action $60.00-70.00

Remington 30 Express, bolt
action . . . . $200.00+

Remington 788, bolt
action $125.00-160.00

Remington 760,
pump $190.00-235.00

Ruger 44, semi-
automatic $145.00-180.00

Savage 99A, lever
action $175.00-215.00

Stevens 26, lever
action $110.00-135.00

Universal Ferret, semi-
automatic $125.00-160.00

Walther KKJ, bolt
action $285.00-360.00

Weatherby Vanguard, bolt
action $270.00-330.00

Western Field 72, lever
action $90.00-110.00

Winchester 60, bolt
action $90.00-110.00

Winchester 490, semi-
automatic $70.00-85.00

Winchester 320, bolt
action $65.00-75.00

Half Dolls

Half dolls are figures that were made to adorn pin cushions, small lamps, candy boxes, powder boxes, clothes brushes, perfume bottles, and other dresser ornaments. Most are made of china, porcelain or bisque and are usually only molded from the waist up. Holes in the base are for sewing. The most sought after half dolls are the ones with arms, flowers and fans molded away from the body. Most are not marked but marked dolls are very desirable, especially those by Dressle, Kister & Company and William Goebel.

China, 2½'', flapper type,
arms over head, marked
German, 1920's . . . $30.00-40.00

China, 4½'', arms away from body with clothes, Germany, late 1800's $50.00-60.00

Bisque on metal stand for lamp, 14'' tall $40.00-50.00

China, 3'', with wig, molded corset, Germany $40.00-50.00

Bisque, child with head band and fan $35.00-50.00

A Dressel and Kister half doll with   headband, worth about $100.00.

146

A half figure made by W. Goebel. $50.00.
This 3¼'' figure is worth about

Hatpin Holders

As hatpins have become more popular, the colorful and attractive hatpin holders have also increased in interest. Though hatpin holders were made in a variety of materials including copper, gold, silver, carnival glass, cut glass, and china, the most popular holders were those of hand-painted porcelain. Many were part of dresser sets, all fashioned in the same material. Beware of reproduction hatpin holders, especially when buying the china type.

R.S. Prussia, painted porcelain,
   handled $135.00-155.00
Royal Bayreuth, painted porcelain,
   vase shape $135.00-145.00
Kewpie, blue
   Jasperware $150.00-175.00
Carnival glass,
   grape and cable .. $125.00-135.00
Figural, owl $135.00-145.00
Figural, pigs at the
   pump $75.00-85.00
Figural, crying babies $45.00-55.00
"Assyrian Gold" $55.00-65.00
Satin Glass, embossed gold
   overlay, 5½" ... $110.00-135.00

Two hatpin holders with a variety of hatpins. On the right is a "Plush Pear" cloth holder valued at $8.00-10.00. The holder on the left is French Ivory (grained celluloid) open mouth holder worth about $15.00-17.00

ed primarily to hold the hat in place they were also very useful for protection. Many are very ornate and contain precious metals and jewels and unusual figures and shapes. The popularity of hatpins declined around the first World War.

A group of Nippon hatpin holders. These handpainted examples from the late 1800's or early 1900's are worth about $55.00-65.00 each.

Figural, Art Deco lady
  in hat $75.00-85.00
Flow blue $30.00-40.00
Heart shape (pin cushion
  type) $9.00-12.00

This silver Indian head figural hatpin is valued at $80.00-95.00.

Hatpins

In the late 1800's as large ornate hats became popular, hatpins to hold them in place also became popular. Though the hatpin was us-

Figural, butterfly,
  with stones $40.00-45.00
Cameo, oval $30.00-35.00
Figural, standing
  monkey $25.00-35.00

149

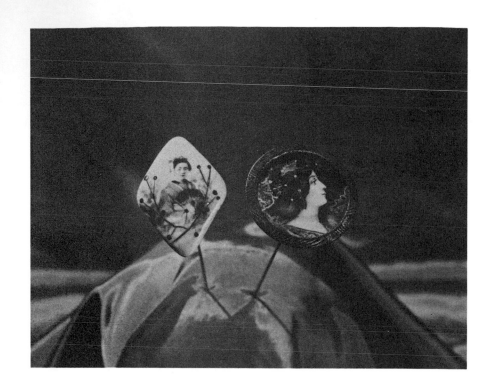

Two transfer portrait hatpins. Each **is valued at $30.00-45.00.**

Figural, rooster
head $30.00-35.00
Carnival Glass,
round $25.00-40.00
Figural,
dragonfly $50.00-60.00
Rhinestone, round,
200 stones $25.00-35.00
Glass, Art Nouveau,
round $30.00-40.00
Souvenir, Niagara
Falls $30.00-35.00
Souvenir, Detroit,
1910 . . . . $30.00-35.00
Figural, Anchor &
USN $30.00-35.00
Milk glass $10.00-20.00
Initial, figural mounting,
lions $20.00-25.00
Figural, Art Deco,
bead and Egyptian
symbol $25.00-30.00

Figural,
elephant $20.00-25.00

Hummel Figurines

The drawings of Sister Maria Innocentia Hummel of the Siessen Convent in Germany have come down to modern day collectors in the form of colorful, lifelike figures produced by the firm of W. Goebel. Hummel figures are very popular today with some rare examples bringing thousands of dollars. Though Hummel figures are still being produced, even new ones are very much in demand by American collectors. The older versions are usually more valuable and collectors are always on the lookout for rare versions and discontinued variations and markings. All genuine Hummel figures are marked, but the collector should

Volunteers

This Hummel figure is titled $110.00+.
"Volunteers" and is valued at

"Little Cellist", $100.00 + .

"Chimney Sweep", $50.00-75.00.

"The Runaway", $100.00-150.00.

"Globe Trotter", $85.00 + .

beware of imitation figures in the same style.

Accordian Boy, 5¼" .... $75.00+
Adoration, 6¼" .... $140.00+
Adventure Bound, large $1500.00+
Angel Serenade, 5".... $125.00+
Angel with Lute,
    small $18.00-20.00
Angelic Care, 6½" .. $55.00-65.00
Angelic Sleep, 4" ... $75.00-135.00
Angelic Song, 4" $80.00-85.00
Apple Tree Boy, 6" .... $110.00+
Apple Tree Girl, 6" .... $110.00+
Baker, 5" .... $60.00+
Barnyard Hero, 4" ...... $75.00+
Begging His Share,
    5½" $85.00-150.00
Be Patient, 4½" .... $70.00+
Birthday Serenade, 4½" . $80.00+
Boots, 6½" .... $225.00+
Boy with Horse, 3½" $20.00-25.00
Boy with Toothache, early,
    5½" .... $100.00+
Boy with Toothache, recent,
    5½" $30.00-45.00
Brother, 5½" .... $70.00+
Builder, 5½" .... $95.00+
Busy Student, 4½" ..... $70.00+
Celestial Musician, 7" $45.00-55.00
Chick Girl, 3½" .... $90.00+
Cinderella, 4½" .... $120.00+
Close Harmony, 5½" .. $120.00+
Confidentially, 5¼" .... $95.00+
Crossroads, 6¾" ...... $180.00+
Culprits, 6½" .... $100.00+
Doctor .... $60.00+
Doll Mother, 4¾" ..... $100.00+
Duet, 5" .... $80.00+
Easter Greetings, 5¼" ... $90.00+
Farm Boy, 5¼" .... $90.00+
Flower Madonna, 8½" . $250.00+
Friends, 11" .... $500.00+
Goose Girl, 4¾" .... $90.00+
Happy Days, 5¼" ..... $95.00+
Hear Ye, 6" .... $90.00+
Heavenly Angel, 6" ..... $85.00+
Heavenly Protection,
    9" $125.00-135.00

Home From Market, 4½" $60.00+
Joyful, 4" $60.00-95.00
Little Helper, 4½" ...... $60.00+
Little Tailor, 5¼" ..... $100.00+
Lullaby, 3¾" $135.00-145.00
Mail Coach .... $300.00+
Max & Moritz, 5¼" ..... $75.00+
Merry Wanderer, 7".... $185.00+
Mischief Maker, 5" .... $100.00+
Mountaineer, 5½" ...... $95.00+
Not For Yur, 6" .... $90.00+
On Secret Path, 5¼" . $45.00-50.00
Prayer Before Battle,
    4½" $65.00-125.00
Retreat to Safety, 4" .... $75.00+
Ring Around the Rosie,
    6¾" .... $1000.00+
Sensitive Hunter, 4¾" .. $250.00+
Signs of Spring, 4" ...... $75.00+
Skier, 5¼" $80.00
Spring Cheer, 5" .... $50.00+
Stormy Weather, 6¼" .. $250.00+
Trumpet Boy, 4¾" .. $70.00-75.00
Village Boy, 5" $35.00-55.00
Viola, 5½" .... $50.00+
Waiter, 6" .... $80.00+
Wayside Harmony, 5" ... $85.00+
We Congratulate, 4" .... $75.00+
Weary Wanderer, 6" .... $80.00+

Indian Artifacts

Indian tools and relics can be found all over the United States and the type of relics found can tell much about the history of a particular area. These items are collected more for their hstoric appeal than their monetary worth. When these tools and relics are uncovered, a record should be kept as to location. This adds to the value and interest of the item. Tools and relics that exhibit good craftsmanship and detail are the most desirable. Geographic boundaries contribute greatly to the value of these items.

Belt, Crow, leather and brass, bead work, 1880s $100.00-125.00

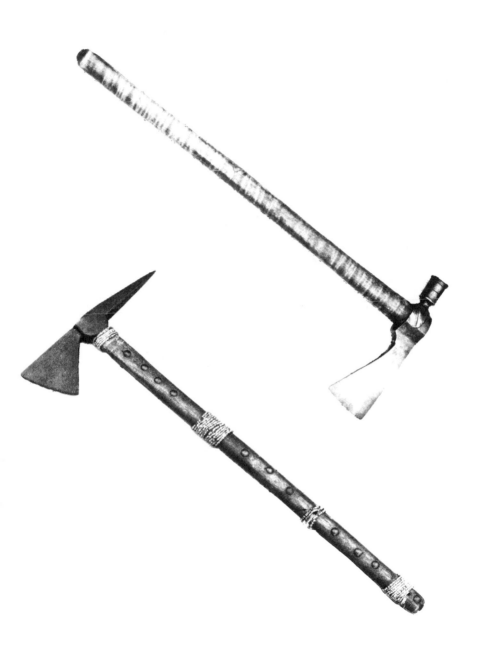

**Iron spike axes, mid 1700's to early
1800's, $600.00+.**

Belt, Sioux, beaded,
28" $200.00-215.00
Armband, beaded on rawhide,
Sioux $60.00-70.00
Baby bonnet, beaded,
Sioux $200.00-250.00
Slate axe, 8½x4¾ . $100.00-115.00
Headband, beaded, Plains
Indians........... $60.00-75.00
Carrying pouch, shaped hide,
Apache $75.00-80.00

This Klamath basket from Southern Oregon from the early 1900's is worth $80.00-110.00.

Toy canoe, 42", bark,
1800's .... $250.00 +
Flute, Sioux........ $60.00-70.00
Bird whistle, pottery . $20.00-30.00
Serape blanket, Navajo,
1880's .... $1000.00 +
Stone elbow pipe,
Pueblo .... $100.00 +
Saddle blanket, beaded, leather,
1880's .... $1000.00 +
Armband, Cheyenne, beaded &
quilled $60.00-70.00
Sweetgrass basket, miniature,
Eastern Woodlands $10.00-15.00

Insulators
Insulator collecting began a few years ago as a spin-off of the bottle and jar collecting hobby. Insulators were introduced in the 1830's for use with telegraph lines and made a transition to telephone lines very easily. Millions of glass insulators were produced in this country from 1850 to 1900 in a variety of colors. Prices here are for unbroken and undamaged insulators. Prices have not risen much in this area in recent years.

Oakman's aqua $75.00
Milford & Biddle,
aqua $25.00-30.00
Mine insulator, aqua . $15.00-18.00
McLaughlin, 42, aqua .. $4.00-6.00
Montreal Telegraph Co.,
aqua $12.00-15.00
Monogram H.I. Co.,
aqua $15.00-20.00
Maydwell, 14, clear,
aqua $3.00-5.00
Macomb, brown pottery $2.00-3.00
Locke, brown pottery .. $1.00-2.00
Liquid Insulator, blue $15.00-20.00
Knowles No. 2 Cable, aqua,
green $25.00-30.00
Hemingray E-1, clear,
yellow $12.00-15.00
H.G. Co., cobalt blue $50.00-60.00
R. Good Jr., aqua $8.00-10.00
W. Brookfield, aqua,
green $1.00-2.00
J.S. Keeling, dark green .. $50.00 +
Postal, aqua $10.00-12.00
Pinco, brown pottery $1.00
Isorex, clear, green, blue,
black $3.00-5.00
California, clear,
amethyst $12.00-15.00
Cable, aqua, green ... $18.00-22.00
Castle, aqua $35.00-40.00
Whitall Tatum #10 aqua,
green $10.00-12.00
Pony, blue $15.00-20.00
Pyrex, clear $1.00-2.00
Sterling, aqua $12.00-15.00
Standard, clear,
amethyst $8.00-10.00

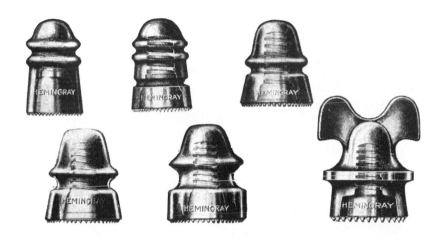

A group of Hemingray glass insulators. Top row from left: No. 9, $1.00-2.50; No. 12, $3.00-5.00; No. 14, $1.00-1.50. Bottom row from left: No. 19, $1.00-2.00; No. 20, $1.00-1.50; No. 60, Mickey Mouse, $12.00-15.00.

Oaki, white pottery .. $35.00-40.00
Tillotson, aqua, green . $8.00-10.00
T.C.R., aqua $8.00-10.00
Westinghouse, #4, aqua,
   green $20.00-25.00
Armstrong 51-3C,
   amber............. $7.00-9.00
Thomas, brown pottery . $3.00-5.00
Noleak, aqua, green .. $25.00-30.00
Otis, purple .... $100.00 +
Agee, clear, amethyst . $10.00-12.00
Birmingham, clear,
   yellow $50.00-60.00
Chambers, aqua $50.00-75.00
Jumbo, aqua $15.00-20.00
Mershon, aqua $25.00-30.00
Santa Anna, aqua,
   green $25.00-30.00

Jewelry

Antique jewelry has increased steadily in value over the past few years. This is due largely to the amount of gold, silver and gems involved. As the prices of modern jewelry continue to climb, people seem to be turning to antique jewelry, causing prices to rise more. Because the valuable metals and gems are involved in jewelry, the prices are rather unstable. Prices can fluctuate greatly in a very short period of time. Jewelry can be a sound investment if only for the amount of valuable elements involved.

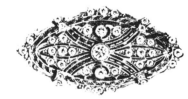

Two pins with diamonds. Each will bring well over $125.00.

159

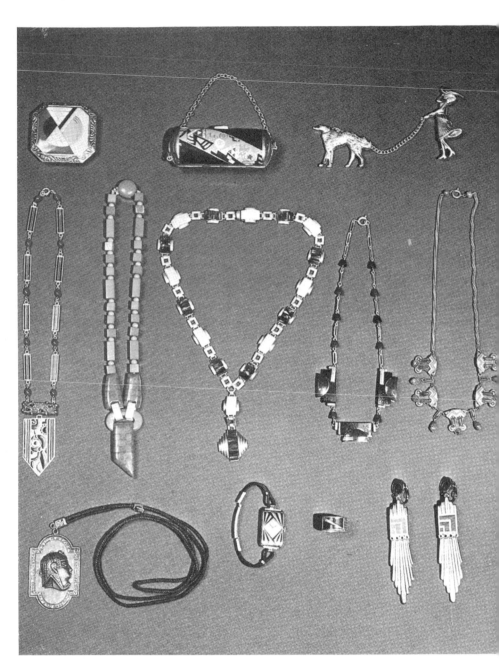

Art Deco Jewelry. Top row: Vanity case, $75.00; vanity case, $125.00; brooch, $25.00. Second row: Necklace, $165.00; necklace, $60.00; necklace, $85.00; necklace, $85.00; necklace, $85.00; Bottom row: Pendant, $55.00; wrist watch, $110.00; ring, $125.00; earrings, $25.00.

Silver jewelry from the 1890's is extremely popular today. Top row left: Chatelaine belt, $400.00; chatelaine belt, $1000.00+; chatelaine belt, $60.00. Bottom row: Coin carrier, $85.00; coin carrier, $55.00; buckles & studs, $400.00.

A group of cameos .

Wedgwood jasperware jewelry.

These purses and handbags from the   about $50.00-100.00 each.
1920's and before would be worth

164

Kestner Dolls

J.D. Kestner was a manufacturer of German dolls in the 19th and early 20th centuries. The company produced many kinds of dolls and most are marked with a crown. Kestner was one of the earlier producers of dolls with sleep eyes. As in the case of all German dolls, Kestner dolls are quite valuable.

A 20½" Kestner doll worth about $150.00-200.00.

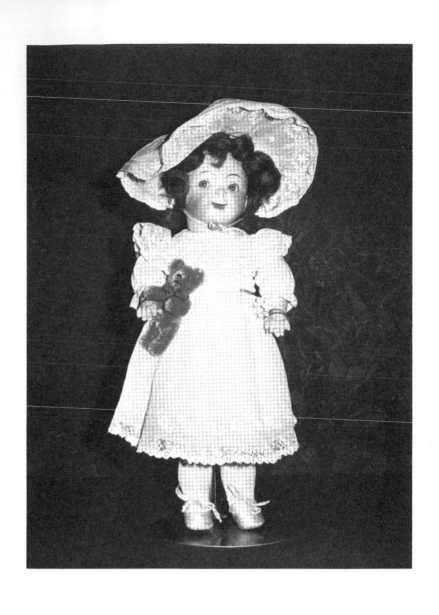

16'' googly Kestner doll, valued at $3000.000.

Bent leg Kestner baby, 18'', $250.00-300.00.

17" shoulder head, sleep eyes,
open mouth . . . . $250.00 +
13" socket head, composition body,
open mouth, set eyes . . $175.00 +
15" shoulder head, bisque
forearms, closed
mouth . . . . $500.00 +
18½" turned shoulder head, sleep
eyes, open mouth . . . . $250.00 +

16" socket head, composition body,
open mouth . . . . $150.00 +
21" socket head, fur eyebrows,
open mouth . . . . $250.00 +
21" socket head, open mouth,
sleep eyes, Daisy . . . . . $175.00 +
10" socket head, open mouth,
baby . . . . $250.00 +

This 18½" Kestner doll is worth   about $250.00-$300.00.

Kitchen Collectibles

Anything used in, or pertaining to, the kitchen is considered a kitchen collectible. This is a wide ranging category that overlaps into other areas of collecting. Most of these items are used solely for decoration. Many pieces, though, such as cabinets, tables, and crockery are being used as functional items. The collector should beware of reproductions in this area.

Dry sink, pine, 1840's,
    plain .... $500.00 +

Lemon squeezer, maple,
    1850's $55.00-70.00
Churn, tin, maple dasher,
    Shaker .... $250.00 +
Slaw cutter, wood,
    1900's $60.00-75.00
Coffee grinder, wall type,
    iron & glass,
    1910 .... $65.00-75.00
Apple peeler, cast iron,
    1900 .... $60.00-70.00
Cherry pitter, 1920's,
    iron $30.00-35.00
Skimmer, brass,
    1840's $100.00-125.00

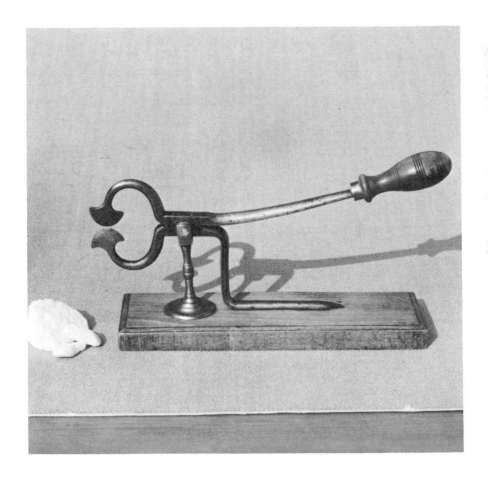

Sugar cutters from the late 1700's or early 1800's, $250.00 + .

Pudding mold, copper,
 1800's $50.00-70.00
Sugar cutter, iron,
 wood base . . . . $250.00 +
Dish drainer, wood,
 handmade $40.00-50.00
Coffee mill, table top, wood,
 brass, iron $150.00-175.00
Cheese knife $25.00-30.00
Apple peeler, wood,
 wheel & pulley . . . . $225.00 +
Ice box, oak $200.00-350.00

This factory made chopping knife with maple handle is from the late 1800's and is worth $35.00-45.00.

Lamps, Electric

The transition to a clean, less troublesome fuel, from the open flame type was welcomed in America. Thomas Edison's patent of the light bulb made it possible to have a more evenly distributed light with only a minimum of preparation and maintenance. Although lighting fixtures have changed outwardly to

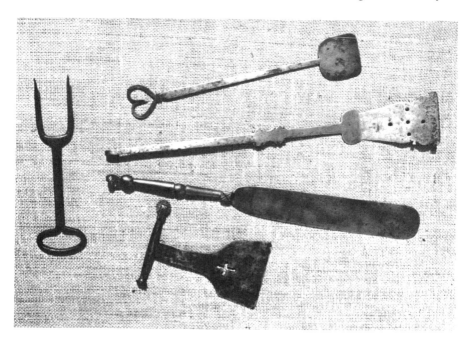

Iron kitchen utensils, left to right: turner, fish slice, spatula, chopper, meat holder. Each is worth around $200.00 except the meat holder which can be found for about $50.00.

Hanging lamp with bent art glass shade, $1000.00 + .

suit the changing tastes of the public, the lamps of today are really not far removed from the early types. Any signed Tiffany lamp will bring from $1000.00 to $10,000.00 and more depending on type and condition. Any Art Nouveau or Art Deco lamps are popular among collectors.

A mission oak lamp, $225.00.

Table lamp, mission
oak $190.00-250.00
Table lamp, brass, triangle, art
glass shade . . . . $300.00 +
Table lamp, urn shape, decorated
globe . . . . $300.00 +
Table lamp, ribbed half globe
shade . . . . $200.00 +
Table lamp, brass, triangle shade
with fringe . . . . $200.00 +
Wall lamp, mission
oak $150.00-175.00
Wall lamp, mission oak, art glass
inserts . . . . $200.00 +
Wall lamp, brass, 3 fixtures, satin
glass shades $175.00-200.00

Dual study lamp, brass,
21'' . . . . $200.00 +
Banquet lamp, white metal and
copper $75.00-85.00
Art deco, reclining nude holding
globe $75.00-100.00
Gone with the Wind, pink with
roses, 26'' tall . . . . . . $275.00 +
Rayo, burnished brass $50.00-75.00
Desk lamp, brass tube, hemisphere
shade, adjustable . . $75.00-90.00
Table lamp, brass base, art glass
hemisphere shade . . . . $225.00 +

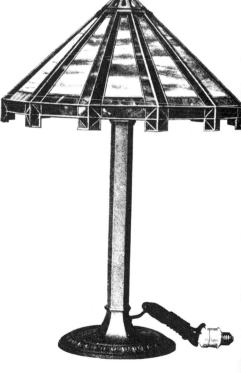

Lamps with art glass shades are very popular. This brass lamp with triangular shade will bring about $300.00.

This bracket type electric lamp with brass base is worth about $50.00.

Lamps, Oil

Oil lamps have been made in many materials, but the majority found today are made of glass. Oil lamps rely on an open flame for light, and have been so popular that they were sold long after electricity was an established form of lighting. Cut and pattern glass lamps made before the turn of the century are very popular, especially the vase or "Gone with the Wind" lamps. The collector should use caution when buying oil lamps because reproductions are available.

Hand lamp, fan pattern,
     1890's $40.00-45.00
Hand lamp, glass, plain,
     saucer base, 1870's . $40.00-50.00
Hand lamp, diamond
     pattern $30.00-35.00

These pan lamps from the 1700's are iron and will bring $80.00 or more.

173

Carnival glass oil lamps.

Hanging, brass, decorated shade, prisms, 1880's ...... $500.00+

Fostoria, satin finish, 1900, vase .... $300.00+

Fostoria, kerosene, roses on base and chimney .... $150.00+

Betty lamp, wrought iron, 1700's $125.00-150.00

Coach lamp, kerosene, tin, glass chimney, 1870's ... $85.00-95.00

Kerosene, tin strap handle, glass chimney, tin shade, 1860's .... $150.00+

Whale oil, flint glass, 1850's .... $225.00+

Whale oil, frosted glass, 8" $50.00-60.00

Hand lamp, glass, plain, 1870's $40.00-45.00

Footed hand lamp, rope pattern, 1870's $40.00-50.00

Gone with the Wind, milk glass .... $300.00+

Miner's lamp, brass, 4" tall $50.00-60.00

Standing, ribbed font . $35.00-45.00

A kerosene miniature lamp from the early 1900's, $100.00.

This tin wall lamp complete with glass chimney was used in the late 1800's, $200.00 + .

Standing, grape band . $45.00-50.00
Hand lamp, shield
    pattern $45.00-50.00
Standing, panel
    pattern $50.00-55.00
Hand lamp, sea shell,
    1860's $35.00-40.00

Limoges

Hard base porcelain is produced by many factories around Limoges, France. The high quality pieces made from the mid 1800's to about 1930 are of interest to antique collectors. Many pieces are artist signed and all are beautiful. There is quite a selection of this porcelain around but nearly all is a premium price.

A handpainted Limoges vase signed "Leona" by Pouyat, $350.00 + .

Mushroom plate, Bawo & Dotter,
    signed "Shuppe" . . $50.00-60.00
Egg plate, Delinieres . $55.00-70.00

This pair of Limoges oyster plates from Bawo & Dotter sells for around $70.00-100.00.

Individual salts, gold border,
GDA $12.00-15.00
Sugar & Creamer, floral, signed
"I.K. Xmas 1894" . $35.00-50.00
Demi-tasse cup,
Pouyat $20.00-25.00
Cider pitcher, roses, signed
"Merenlet" $135.00-160.00
Lemonade pitcher, grapes, Kittle
& Klingenberg . . . $165.00-195.00
Berry set, serving bowl and 6
smaller bowls, floral and
birds $95.00-135.00
Tobacco jar, pipe on lid, mountain
scene $155.00-185.00
Ewer, pansies, Kittle &
Klingenberg $55.00-75.00
Candleholder, signed "L.E. Miller,
Xmas '07" $45.00-65.00
Cachepot, signed "M.
Dorothy" . . . . $350.00+

Dresser tray, Vignaud $40.00-60.00
Hand mirror, floral,
T & V $35.00-50.00
Trinket box, Limoges
France $45.00-65.00

Locks

Locks of wood crossbars were used in Egypt and biblical cities. Since that time locksmithing has evolved to our present day sophisticated lock mechanisms. Old locks and keys are of interest to collectors if they are in good condition and working order. Railroad locks are especially popular.

Military gun rack lock, screw
key $25.00-35.00
German, ward lock $5.00-6.00
Sprocket, ward lock . . $20.00-25.00

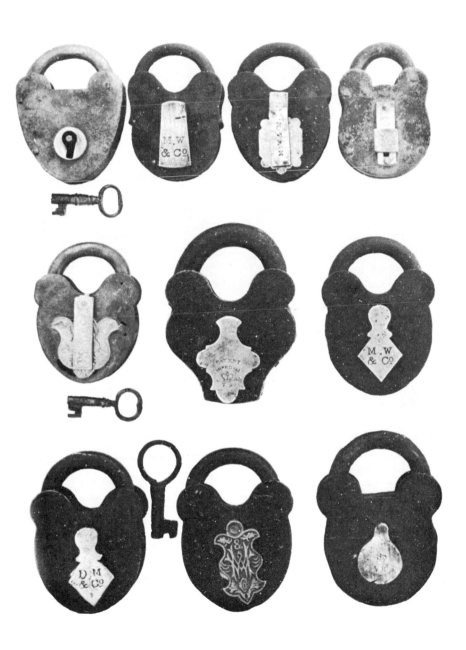

A group of wrought iron ward $15.00-20.00.
locks. Each is worth about

Slaymaker, ward lock,
"York" $6.00-7.00
Lion, wafer lock $4.00-5.00
U.S. Mail, two lever
lock $7.00-15.00
Keen Kutter, six lever
lock $35.00-50.00
Simmons Wireless, six lever
lock $15.00-20.00
M.W. & Co., wrought iron, ward
lock $15.00-20.00
J.C. Higgins, ward lock $6.00-7.00

Madame Alexander Dolls

Madame Alexander dolls are probably the most collected dolls in the world. Hundreds of different dolls have been designed by Madame Alexander in the past 52 years, giving the collector a very wide range from which to choose. Prices here are for dolls in mint or near mint condition. Dolls in original boxes would be valued slightly higher.

Amish boy, 8'', 1960 ... $300.00+
Apple Annie, Americana, 8'',
1954 .... $225.00+
Baby Jane, 16'', 1935 ... $400.00+
Beauty Queen, 1961 $125.00-140.00
Carrot Top, 21'',
1967 .... $60.00-70.00
Davy Crockett, 8'', 1955 $300.00+
Eskimo, 8'', 1960's ..... $300.00+
Faith, 8'' Americana,
1961 .... $200.00+
Gold Rush, 11'', 1963 ... $800.00+
Happy, 20'', 1970 .... $80.00-90.00
Ice Skater, 8'', 1950 .... $175.00+
Jogo Slav, 7'', 1930's $100.00
King, 21'', 1940's ...... $400.00+
Lazy Mary, 7'', 1930's .. $100.00+
Maid of Honor, 18'' .... $175.00+
Nan McDare .... $125.00+
Orphan Annie, 14'',
1965 .... $200.00+
Parlour Maid, 8'', 1956 . $300.00+
Queen, 18'', 1953 ...... $250.00+
Rozy, 12'', 1969 .... $125.00+

Dionne Quints. This set of Madame Alexander dolls in the original wood bed would sell for over $500.00.

178

Madame Alexander dolls. Bill & Wendy from the 1950's worth over $150.00 each.

This Madame Alexander 14'' Soldier doll from 1942 is worth about $175.00.

Shari Lewis, 14'', 1959 .. $175.00 +
Three Pigs & Wolf,
    1938 .... $300.00 each
Victorian, 18'', 1953 .... $300.00 +
Wendy Angel, 8''
    1954 .... $300.00 +

Magazines

Old magazines give the collector a look at how life was in the past. The cost of magazines in good condition is increasing, especially those before 1920, World War II issues, and some issues with special historical significance. There is a variety of magazines available to the collector on many subjects. Discontinued publications are very popular and demand good prices but early issues of Playboy are probably the most sought after magazines with the December 1953 issue worth over $500.00.

179

American, 1940's $1.00-1.50	Builder, 1850's $2.00-4.00
American Home, Pinocchio issue,	Cosmopolitan, 1890's $15.00-20.00
1939 .... $2.50-3.50	Country Home, 1930's . $ .50-1.00
American Needlewoman,	Everybody's, 1920's $2.50-3.00
1930's.............. $ .50-1.00	Field & Stream, 1900's .. $2.00-3.00

This war years issue, December 1942   is valued at $4.00-$5.00.

Good Housekeeping with
Disney page $5.00-6.00

The first issue of Life Magazine, November 23, 1936. Today this issue will bring $50.00-75.00 from serious collectors.

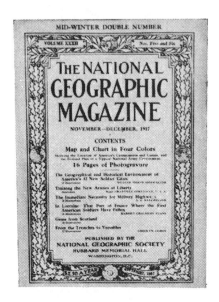

This National Geographic double number is worth about $10.00.

Holiday, 1940's $2.00-4.50
Hunter, Trader, Trapper,
   before 1900 .... $4.00-5.00
Ladies Home Journal,
   1920's $1.00-4.00
Lumber Trade Journal,
   1890's $1.00-2.00
McCalls, 1880's $5.00-8.00
Outing, 1870's $30.00-40.00
Popular Mechanics, 1940's$.50-1.00
Redbook, 1930's....... $2.00-4.00
Smart Set, 1930's $1.00-1.25
Travel, 1940's .... $ .50-1.00
Womans World, 1930's . $1.00-2.00
Yankee, 1940's .... $ .50-1.00

Marbles

The game of marbles is one of the oldest in history. Over the years many types of marbles have been made: sulphides, swirls, stone, crockery, china, clay, and other materials. Marbles are popular with collectors and because of the bright cheerful colors make attractive displays. The most sought after marble is probably the sulphide. The large sulphides with double figures will easily bring over $100.00 from a marble collector.

Stone Marbles

	½"	¾"	1"
Common	$3.00	$3.50	$7.00
Agate	$15.00	$7.50	$12.50
Tiger Eye	$17.50	$12.50	$27.50

Unglazed China

	½"	¾"	1"
Lines	$1.50	$1.25	$2.00
Bullseye	$1.75	$1.50	$2.25
Leaves	$1.75	$2.00	$2.00

Sulphides

Double figures	$100.00-125.00
Animals	$50.00-75.00
Train	$50.00-75.00
Color figures	$100.00-$125.00

Swirls

Banded	$6.50	$3.00	$12.50
Split Core	$4.75	$4.50	$12.50
Candle	$4.50	$5.00	$12.50
Candy	$4.50	$4.75	$12.50
Joseph	$12.50	$7.50	$17.50

Glazed China

Lines	$2.00	$3.00	$4.75
Bullseye	$2.00	$1.75	$3.00
Leaves	$2.00	$2.00	$3.00
Stars	$3.00	$2.75	$5.50
Flowers	$3.25	$3.25	$5.50

Crockery or Bennington

Brown	$1.00	$1.00	$2.50
Speckled	$1.25	$1.50	$3.00
Blue	$1.00		$2.75
Odd color	$2.00	$2.00	$4.00

McCoy Pottery

McCoy Pottery has become increasingly popular with collectors in recent years, with some of the more rare hand painted pieces selling for hundreds of dollars. The most abundant products of McCoy are the popular cookie jars but the most

McCoy art pottery from the Loy-Nel-Art line about 1905. Top row: jardiniere, $30.00-40.00; 11'' vase, $80.00-90.00; 6'' vase, $60.00-80.00. Middle row: jardiniere, $150.00 + ; 9'' vase, $80.00-90.00; jardiniere, $60.00-80.00. Bottom row: bowl, $60.00-80.00; bowl, $80.00-$90.00; bowl $60.00-80.00.

McCoy cookie jars. Picnic basket 1960's, $15.00-20.00; Cabin, 1950's, $14.00-18.00; Floral, 1940's, $10.00-12.00; Dutch boy, 1940's $10.00-12.00; Mammy, 1940's & 1950's, $10.00-$15.00; Teapot, 1971, $7.00-10.00.

McCoy vases from the 1940's and 1950's worth about $5.00-8.00 each.

desirable pieces are the hand painted pieces from the early 1900's. As the rare types increase in value, all kinds of McCoy pottery are being grabbed up by collectors.

Vase, Rosewood, 9'' . $20.00-40.00
Vase, 11'', Olympian ... $125.00 +
Ewer, Mt. Pelee........ $175.00 +
Candlesticks, Onyx .. $18.00-25.00
Jardiniere, 4''
   Hayley's Comet ..... $150.00 +
Tilt pitcher, 1930's,
   floral $18.00-22.00

Uncle Sam Vase, 1940's $8.00-10.00
Indian, cookie jar,
   1950's........... $50.00-60.00
Elephant, pitcher,
   1940's........... $18.00-22.00
Donkey, pitcher,
   1940's........... $18.00-22.00
Pig planter, 1940's $3.00-5.00
Ducks & eggs, planter .. $3.00-5.00
Panther planter,
   1940's........... $10.00-15.00
Ram's head vase,
   1940's........... $12.00-18.00
Humpty Dumpty planter $3.00-5.00

185

Safe, cookie jar,
  1960's $12.00-15.00
Strawberry, cookie jar,
  1950's $12.00-15.00
Rocking Chair Dalmations,
  cookie jar, 1962 . . . $25.00-30.00
Christmas Tree, cookie jar
  1950's $30.00-40.00
Lollipop, cookie jar,
  1950's $12.00-15.00

Medical Collectibles

Medical collectibles are fast becoming of major interest in the area of collecting, especially to those that have some interest in the medical field. Although many of the items considered medical collectibles were actually used by doctors, dentists, nurses or hospitals, this is not the rule, Many in fact, are pharmaceutical items from druggists and drug stores or items sold as home remedies or cures. Anything from bottled pills to electric shocking machines is popular including the "quack" pieces that were originally sold promising miraculous cures.

Vapor lamp $30.00-35.00
Inhaler, China,
  blue and white $45.00-60.00
Electromagnetic machine,
  wood case . . . . $125.00 +
Bath thermometer, glass
  and wood $20.00-30.00

Medical collectibles, left to right: eye cup.
Chill tonic glass; mortal and pestle,

These glassine label bottles are worth about $20.00-25.00 each.

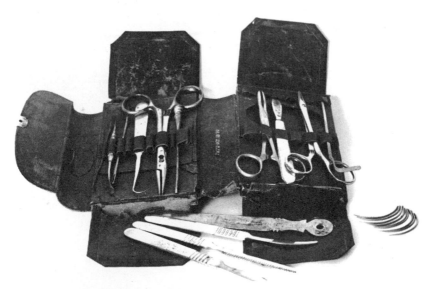

A surgeon's kit in leather pouch from the 1890's.

Cork press, iron $30.00-40.00
Ear trumpet......... $30.00-40.00
Microscope, brass,
    1800's .... $200.00 +
Dental hand tools
    1900's.............. $3.50-5.00
Bleeder, brass,
    folding $30.00-40.00
Homeopathic kit, pocket,
    1900 .... $10.00-12.00
Table mold, 1890's $8.00-10.00
Mortar and Pestle,
    brass............. $20.00-40.00
Compound press, brass,
    1870's .... $200.00 +
Violet ray machine ... $25.00-35.00
M. Thurlow's Homeopathic
    Medicine Chest,
    wood case.......... $200.00 +
Graduated scale, 4 oz.,
    1890's.............. $5.00-7.50
Doctor's bag,
    alligator $40.00-50.00
Portable prescription scale,
    1880's............ $60.00-70.00

Surgeon's kit, 1890's, leather
    case and tools $50.00-75.00
Stethescope, 1890,
    wood earpiece $60.00-75.00

Nazi Collectibles

Items used by the Third Reich are popular with collectors today, especially those used during battle. Medals, daggers, uniform decorations and insignias are all very popular. The collector should be careful to avoid reproductions and faked items in this field.

Dress uniform, Luftwaffe
    pilot .... $150.00 +
Dagger, Luftwaffe
    officer's .... $175.00 +
Helmet, steel,
    Afrikakorps......... $175.00 +
Clock, Navy submarine . $500.00 +
Pocket knife, Nazi
    party .... $150.00 +
Hat, diplomatic corps.. $1000.00 +

This Navy Captain's hat is worth about $500.00.

Hand grenade, wood
   handle $65.00-75.00
Utility knife,
   paratrooper .... $150.00+
Badge, glider pilot..... $1000.00+
Hat, railroad
   conductor's $75.00-100.00
Badge, cloth, Navy High
   Seas $75.00-100.00
Badge, patrol boat ..... $200.00+
Badge, Navy
   destroyer $60.00-75.00

A numbered Tank Assault badge, 25 assaults, $250.00.

Cap badge, cloth Eagle,
   Luftwaffe $100.00-150.00
Sleeve patch, S.S.
   guard $50.00-70.00
Medal, Customs Service
   decoration $100.00-125.00
Medal, Civilian Shooting
   badge $25.00-50.00
Hat, General's visor ... $1000.00+
Helmet, paratrooper,
   camouflage cover $200.00-250.00
Badge, Condor Legion,
   tank .... $700.00+

Nippon

Hand painted pieces of porcelain imported into this country from Japan from 1890 to 1921 were marked "Nippon". These colorful inexpensive pieces that have now become quite popular and many have become relatively expensive. There are many examples and varities available to the collector.

Potpourri jar, floral
   design........... $90.00-120.00
Sugar and creamer,
   roses $60.00-85.00
Lamp, 17" tall, Oriental boat
   scene $175.00-250.00
Humidor, bulldog . $275.00-350.00
Whiskey jug, fox hunt .. $300.00+
Chocolate set, roses $275.00-325.00
Pancake server,
   floral $85.00-115.00
Slanted cheese dish .. $90.00-135.00
Loving cup vase,
   windmill $65.00-90.00
Compote, floral $70.00-100.00

Nippon vase, $200.00 or more.

Nippon porcelain cookie jar, $250.00 +, and cake plate, $150.00 +.

Oak

Oak furniture has become one of the most popular types of antique furniture available today. Its sturdy construction combined with the solidness of the wood give it the ability to stand up for years. There are two main types of Oak, regular sawed and quarter sawed. The quarter sawed wood gives the furniture's grain a "radiating" look. Prices here are for furniture that is excellent quality, refinished and restored.

Folding bed . . . . $400.00 +
Book Case, 1 door,
   glass $150.00-175.00
Book case, 2 doors,
   glass . . . . $400.00 +
Book case, sectional . . . . $300.00 +
Buffet $250.00-500.00
China Buffet . . . . $400.00 +
Chairs, dining, cane seats,
   set of four . . . . $300.00 +
Chairs, dining, leather bottom,
   set of four . . . . $300.00 +
Chairs, dining, wood seat,
   set of four . . . . $300.00 +

Chairs, kitchen, cane seats,
   set of four . . . . $250.00 +
Chairs, kitchen, leather seats,
   set of four . . . . $250.00 +
Chairs, kitchen, wood seats,
   set of four . . . . $175.00 +
Desk chair, swivel . . $125.00-200.00
Desk chair, straight . $50.00-100.00
Rocking chair,
   carved $150.00-175.00
Rocking chair, plain . . $60.00-80.00

This ornate oak bed is worth $500.00.

Rocking chair,
upholstered $110.00-180.00
Rocking chair,
cane seat $150.00-200.00
Children's rocking chair,
carved $100.00-150.00
Children's rocking chair,
plain $50.00-75.00
Chiffonier $125.00-200.00
Chifforobe $100.00-140.00
China cabinet,
glass front . . . . $500.00+
China cabinet, small,
plain . . . . $300.00+
Couch . . . . $400.00+
Davenport . . . . $250.00+
Desk, small ladies . . . . . . $300.00+
Desk, drop front . . . . $225.00+

Desk, small
missionary $125.00-150.00
Desk, large rolltop . . . . $1200.00+
Desk, small rolltop . . . . . $250.00+
Desk, stand-up . . . . $300.00+
Dresser . . . . $200.00+
Dresser, Princess . . . . $175.00+
Dresser, small,
plain . . . . $125.00+
Hall rack, with seat . . . . . $450.00+
Hall rack, with seat,
small . . . . $300.00+
Kitchen cabinet . . . . $200.00+
Kitchen cabinet with leaded
glass . . . . $350.00+
Kitchen cabinet with
frosted glass . . . . $350.00+
Stand-up mirror . . . . $185.00+

Oak sectional bookcase and detail of assembly, a five section case usually costs between $300.00 and $375.00.

Kitchen cabinets, $350.00-400.00.

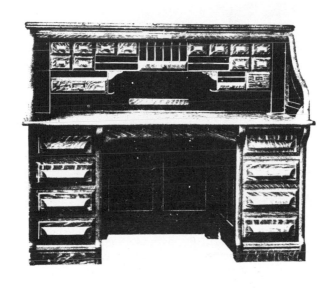

Oak Roll Top desks, 1000.00 each.

Round oak tables are choice pieces. This type with carved claw feet br-ings $450.00 or more.

Hanging mirror $35.00-65.00
Kitchen table $75.00-100.00
Round pedestal table ... $300.00 +
Round pedestal table
   with claw feet .... $375.00 +
Stand table $75.00-100.00
End table $50.00-80.00
Wash stands $130.00-170.00
Oval mirror $40.00-50.00
Shaving mug rack ..... $220.00 +

Barber's cabinet .... $200.00 +
Medicine cabinet $35.00-50.00
Music cabinet .... $100.00 +
Wardrobe .... $200.00 +
Pedestal, ornate $75.00-90.00
Pedestal, plain $50.00-60.00
Stool, swivel with
   back $100.00-200.00
Stool, swivel,
   no back $80.00-100.00

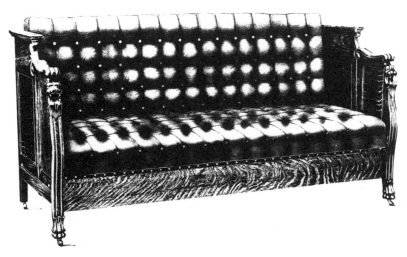

This oak davenport with lion heads and leather upholstery is valued at $400.00.

Stool $65.00-85.00
Card file cabinet,
   8 drawer $170.00-190.00
Card file cabinet,
   with roll front .... $300.00 +
Dish cupboard,
   glass doors .... $325.00 +
Dish cupboard,
   no glass .... $200.00 +
Sleigh bed .... $250.00 +
Settee .... $250.00 +
Ice box, 75 lb. .... $200.00 +

A chest type oak ice box, $200.00-225.00.

Oak rockers are plentiful and popular, an example like this usually can be found for $120.00-140.00.

Ice box, 100 lb. .... $300.00 +
Ice box, chest type ...... $200.00 +
Dining table, square .... $150.00 +
Library table, oval ..... $175.00 +
Round end table $60.00-80.00
Umbrella stand $45.00-60.00
Piano bench $70.00-80.00
Piano stool $70.00-80.00
Mirror with shelf ... $95.00-110.00

Occupied Japan

Following World War II anything made for export in Japan during the American Occupation had to be marked either "Occupied Japan" or "Made in Occupied Japan." Since this occupation lasted only about 8 years, the items manufactured and exported at that time have become collectors items. Many products were made during this period including those manufactured of glass, celluloid, metal, paper, and wood. Because there is such an abundance of available collectibles, the value of Occupied Japan is relatively low. But as more collectors begin to surface the collectibles are already increasing in value.

Toy Village $20.00-25.00
Football player, figure,
   wood $7.50-9.00
Wind-up Chevrolet, tin, in
   box $10.00-12.00
Wind-up Studebaker, tin, in
   box $10.00-12.00
Dagger, rubber $6.00-7.00
Checkers, in box,
   wood $10.00-12.00

Occupied Japan workhorse and chicken, $7.00 each.

Japanese dolls, in box $35.00-40.00
Tea Set, Donald Duck 4 place
    setting, in box $30.00-35.00
Doll House, 3-piece bath
    set $15.00-20.00
Dinnerware, Wild Rose, Fuji, 4
    place setting $75.00-100.00
Dinnerware, Forget-Me-Not,
    Aladdin $75.00-100.00
Fishbowl figure, frog . $10.00-12.00
Fishbowl figure,
    mermaid $10.00-12.00
Fishbowl figure, ship . . . $6.00-7.50
Fishbowl figure, arches . $7.00-9.00
Wind chimes, glass . . . $15.00-20.00
Glass animals, small $6.00-6.50
Girl with egg timer $8.00-10.00
Lacquerware tray, 5
    part $45.00-50.00
Lacquerware goblet $5.00-7.50
Lacquerware, cup &
    saucer $8.00-12.00
Lamp, Wedgewood
    style $45.00-50.00
Pincushion, 12
    "coolies" $15.00-17.00
Needle assortment $3.00-5.00
Picnic basket $45.00-50.00
Cigarette dispenser,
    wood $15.00-17.00
Bamboo dipper $15.00-17.00

Occupied Japan dolls, $35.00-40.00.

Salt & Pepper, Toby
    Mug $15.00-17.00
Telephone cigarette lighter,
    metal $15.00-17.00

10½'' Chinese Opera doll $100.00.

14" 19th Century Imari From Japan $275.00.

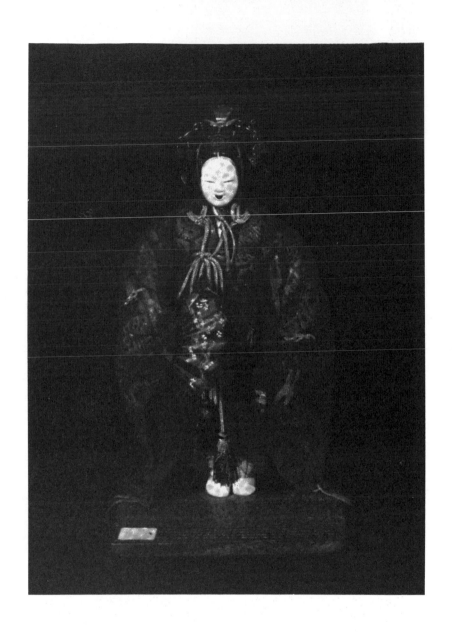

10'' Japanese Kabuki dancer $65.00-70.00.

10'' Chinese baby, 1930's $30.00-35.00.

Oriental Dolls

Many unusual and interesting dolls have been produced in China, Japan, Korea, Thailand, and other Oriental countries. These dolls range from simple folk figures to very detailed pieces of art and the price range corresponds.

China, cloth 5-doll family,
  silk faces $20.00-25.00
China, 10" baby, 1930's,
  composition $30.00-35.00
China, boy and girl, cloth and
  composition $80.00-90.00
China, boy with sock cap,
  composition, current $8.00-10.00
Japan, 13" country boy, stuffed
  and composition,
  1950's $120.00-130.00

Japan, Madame Butterfly, wire
  and cloth, 13" $35.00-40.00
Japan, dancer, "Maiko San", wire
  and cloth, 16" $18.00-25.00
Vietnam, wire and cloth,
  18" $5.00-10.00
Korea, 8" woman, wire
  and cloth $7.00-10.00
Korea, wire and cloth, 16½"
  dancer $8.00-10.00

Paper Dolls

Dolls of paper, either complete booklets or magazine pages are highly collectible. The dolls here are booklets and priced for complete uncut examples. Celebrities and dolls from movies are the most popular paperdolls at this time, but all types are collectible.

Old Japanese warrior dolls. These have clay composition faces, cloth bodies and wood hands and feet. **They stand about 8" tall and are valued at about $225.00.**

Tom the Aviator, a 1941 Lowe paper doll book sells for about $8.00-$10.00.

<u>Saalfield</u>
Gloria Jean, 1940 .... $25.00-35.00
Comics Paper Dolls,
  1935 .... $75.00.00 +

Charlie Chaplin & Paulette
  Goddard, 1941 ..... $75.00.00 +
Circus Paper Dolls,
  1952 .... $7.00-10.00

The Merrill Janet Leigh paperdoll **book from 1953 is worth $35.00.**

This Arlene Dahl paperdoll book from Saalfield, 1953, can be found for $25.00.

Double Date, 1957 . . . . . $3.00-5.00
Marilyn Monroe, 1953 . . . $50.00 +
Sandra Dee, 1959 . . . . $15.00
Blondie, 1968 . . . . $4.00-6.00
Little Women, 1960 . . . $8.00-12.00
Texas Rose, 1959 . . . . . $8.00-12.00

Lowe
Twinkle Twins, 4 Years Old,
 1944 . . . . $4.00-6.00
Career Girls, 1950 . . . . $8.00-12.00
Fashion Previews, 1949 $8.00-12.00
Harry The Soldier,
 1941 . . . . $6.00-10.00
Lollipop Kids, 1961 . . . . $1.00-3.00
Janet Leigh, 1957 . . . . $20.00-30.00
Baby Doll, 1957 . . . . $3.00-5.00
Patti Page, 1957 . . . . . $20.00-30.00
Little Girls, 1969 . . . . . . $1.00-2.00

Merrill
Esther Williams, 1950 $30.00-40.00
Betty Grable, 1953 . . . $30.00-40.00
Ranch Family, 1957 . . . . $4.00-6.00
Gone with the Wind,
 1940 . . . . $75.00 +
Grown Up, 1936 . . . . . $15.00-25.00

Cowboy and Cowgirl,
 1950 . . . . $4.00-6.00
Double Wedding,
 1939 . . . . $20.00-30.00
Liberty Belles, 1943 . . $12.00-17.00
Sonja Henie, 1940 . . . . $75.00 +
Rita Hayworth, 1942 . . . . $60.00 +

Pattern Glass
Pattern glass is clear glass with designs pressed into the glass. There are hundreds of patterns from which to choose and many pieces in each pattern. Prices vary due to scarcity and popularity of patterns as well as individual pieces.

Acorn, goblet $25.00-40.00
Ball, pitcher $30.00-50.00
Cable, decanter $60.00-75.00
Daisy & Scroll, salt
 shaker $7.00-12.00
Empire, butter dish . . $15.00-25.00
Fan Band, sugar
 bowl $12.00-25.00
Garland, mug $16.00-22.00
Harp, compote $75.00-150.00

Intaglio, syrup	$12.00-20.00
Lakewood, jam jar	$12.00-20.00
Nail, goblet	$23.00-45.00
Owl & Fan, relish dish	$15.00-25.00
Ring & Block, plate	$12.00-20.00
Sheild, goblet	$15.00-22.00
Texas Star, pitcher	$30.00-50.00

Actress Chain goblet, worth $45.00-65.00.

Angora goblet, worth $10.00-15.00.

Peanut Collectibles

Peanut machines were once as evident as the gumball machine. The old machines now bring good prices as do other collectibles related to peanuts and peanut companies. By far the most popular are Planter's items and the dapper "Mr. Peanut". Dolls, banks, salt shakers, jars, and many other items are available in this area. Some premiums are still being produced today.

Planter's "Mr. Peanut" salt & pepper and figure. Many plastic items are still available. 50¢-1.00 each.

Peanut vendor machine, 11" tall $35.00

Peanut jar, Squirrel,
glass $20.00-22.50
Peanut jar, Planters, peanut
engraving, glass ... $70.00-80.00
Doll, Planters, "Mr. Peanut",
wood $35.00-50.00
Machine, 1¢ Northwestern Co.,
glass & metal $100.00-115.00
Salt & Pepper, "Mr.
Peanut".......... $7.50-15.00
Machine, 1¢ Advance,
1920's $85.00-110.00
Tin, Robinson Crusoe Peanuts,
cylinder .... $100.00+
Peanut jar, Elephant Peanuts,
embossed elephant $75.00-100.00

Tin, Mammoth Salted Peanuts,
cylinder $40.00-50.00
Peanut Vendor, metal and glass
on base, 11" tall ... $15.00-25.00
Peanut jar, Gordons Peanuts,
panel truck, glass .. $15.00-20.00
Planters, nut set, tin bowls,
5 pieces $10.00-15.00

Philatelics

Philatelics, stamp collecting, is one
of the largest collecting hobbies in
existence. Postage stamps offer a
colorful, historical look at the
United States or the entire world.

These two early western letters were
carried and cancelled by Wells
Fargo & Co. The letter at the top is
valued at $35.00-65.00, the bottom
letter, $50.00-75.00.

Many collectors specialize in one or more areas of this emense hobby while others collect a cross section of many types. There are some very scarce and valuable stamps but most are worth only a few cents. The material here is generally philatelic related items that have an historic or nostalgic interest as well. In spite of the many collectors, many bargains are still to be found in old papers, documents, etc.

Graf Zeppelin stamp and
   postmarked cover,
   1930 .... $300.00 +
Cover postmarked Boston &
   Albany R.R. 1853 ..... $25.00 +
Cover postmarked South
   Minnesota R.R.,
   1872 .... $12.00-17.00
Newspaper stamp, $60.00, Indian
   girl, used .... $150.00 +
Souvenir sheet, 3¢ and 8¢, Liberty,
   used, late 1800's $1.00-2.00
Letter with Chicago Shield,
   cancellation $30.00
Graf Zeppelin stamp,
   $1.30, unused ...... $1000.00 +
Cover or card with R.P.O.
   postmark $2.00-5.00
Cover, steamboat stationery
   with steamboat postmark,
   1870's .... $55.00 +
Cover, steamboat, postmark
   and cancellation, 1870's .. $35.00

Phonograph Records

Phonograph records have blossomed into popular collectibles in recent years. Most were produced in large enough quantities to be readily available to collectors in search of past favorites. The records with the largest followings are the old 78 R.P.M.'s and the 45 R.P.M. recordings of more recent times. Desirable records are those with popular recording stars on now extinct labels, or recording groups featuring later popular individual artists. Since the death of Bing Crosby, his recordings, especially early ones, have increased considerably in value. The same is true of the records of Elvis Presley. The 45's most in demand are produced from 1950-65.

78 RPM
Louis Armstrong, Columbia,
   "Star Dust" $7.00-12.00
Cab Calloway,
   Brunswick, ... $5.00-10.00
Bing Crosby, Columbia, "My Kind
   of Love" $8.00-12.00
Jimmy Dorsey, Okeh, "Praying the
   Blues" $7.00-10.00
Tommy Dorsey, Okeh, "Tiger
   Ray" $8.00-12.00
Duke Ellington, Blu Disc, "Rose
   Marie".......... $20.00-30.00
Judy Garland, Decca ... $4.00-7.00
George Gershwin,
   Columbia $5.00-8.00
Benny Goodman, Brunswick,
   "Jungle Blues" $15.00
Lionel Hampton, Victor $3.00-5.00
Harry James, Columbia $4.00-7.00
Glenn Miller, Brunswick, "I Got
   Rhythm" $7.00-12.00
Mills Brothers, Brunswick, "Smoke
   Rings" $7.00-10.00
Artie Shaw, Brunswick $5.00-10.00
Sophie Tucker,
   Columbia $4.00-8.00
45 RPM
The Beach Boys, Candix,
   "Surfin" $40.00-60.00
The Cadillacs, Capitol, "White
   Gardenia" $6.00-10.00
Johnny Cash, Sun, "Hey
   Porter" $5.00-8.00
Ray Charles, Atlantic, "The
   Midnight Hour".... $8.00-12.00
The Dells, Vee Jay, "Tell The
   World" .... $200.00 +
Little Jimmy Dickens, Columbia,
   "Rock Me"........ $7.00-10.00

An album of Louis Armstrong records. These recordings are reissues and sell for $5.00-7.00 each.

Satchmo's records on Okeh 78's will bring $10.00-$15.00 each.

Fats Domino, Imperial, "How Long" $15.00-20.00
Imperials, Savoy, "My Darling" $75.00-100.00
B.B. King, Kent $3.00-6.00
Jerry Lee Lewis, Sun, "Crazy Arms" $5.00-8.00
Muddy Waters, Chess, "Oh Yeah" $8.00-12.00
Ricky Nelson, Imperial, "Stood Up" $7.00-10.00
Carl Perkins, Sun, "Gone Gone Gone" $15.00-20.00

Ray Smith, Sun $4.00-7.00
Solitaires, Old Town, "My Dear" $8.00-12.00
Valentines, Ramco, "Christmas Prayer" $20.00-30.00
Youngsters, Empire, "Shattered Dreams" $8.00-12.00
Bo Diddley, Checker ... $3.00-5.00

Phonographs

The phonograph was first patented in the late 1870's and was known as the "talking machine". Cylinders, discs and records were used on the early machines and a variety of speaker devices were tried. Nearly all early types and brands of phonographs are popular today with collectors paying high prices for those in excellent condition. The prices here are for those that are in working order with no missing parts either in the working mechanism or the decorative cabinet.

Climax, disc phonograph $150.00+
Victor II with horn ..... $300.00+
Edison, Fireside,
   cylinder type .... $225.00+
Edison, Amberola...... $175.00+
Edison, Home model ... $150.00+
Victor, R Model,
   with horn .... $275.00+
Royal, Talking Machine,
   with horn .... $250.00+
Victor, Model E
   with horn .... $150.00+

A third model Victor phonograph with crank and flower horn. Made around 1900, this type of phonograph is popular and will bring $350.00 or more.

208

American Standard
   with horn .... $200.00 +
Victor, Victrola,
   oak cabinet .... $200.00 +
Edison, Maroon Gem
   with horn .... $650.00 +
Mikiphone, portable ... $150.00 +
Columbia, Eagle,
   with horn .... $150.00 +

Photography

Cameras & Equipment

Cameras have become increasingly popular among collectors in recent years. There are hundreds of cameras and photographic equipment available to collectors today, due to the relative newness of the hobby. Age is not always the value determining factor when dealing in photography equipment and prices tend to fluctuate greatly in this area. Values are for cameras in good condition.

Kodak Boy Scout Camera,
   1930's $30.00-35.00
Argus C2 35MM,
   1930's $15.00-25.00
Ansco Vest Pocket No. 1,
   1912 .... $15.00-20.00
Autograflex Jr., 4 x 5,
   1915 .... $60.00-75.00
Cartridge Kodak, No. 4,
   1890's $80.00-95.00
Zeiss Contaflex,
   1930's $325.00-375.00
Super Kodak Six-20,
   1930's .... $750.00 +
Scovill & Adams, Detective
   Camera, 1880's wood
   box .... $500.00 +
Kodak Panorama
   No. 1 .... $75.00-125.00
Steinheil Tropical
   Camera .... $250.00 +
Kodak Girl Scout,
   1930's $50.00-65.00
Brownie Kodak Stereo No. 2,
   early 1900's $180.00-200.00

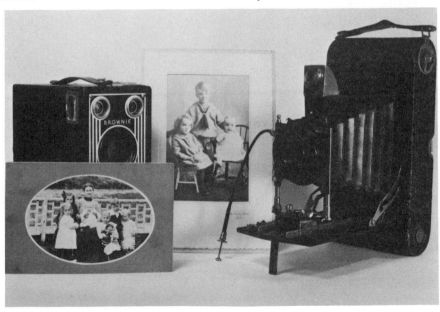

A Kodak Autographed Folding Camera from 1914 worth about $30.00-35.00, and a brownie from the 1950's worth about $5.00-10.00. The photographs date from the late 1800's or early 1900's.

A comedy studio-cabinet view.

American Indian woman.

Occupational Studio/Cabinet view.

A military view.

Kodak Vest Pocket,
1917 . . . . $45.00-60.00
Stereo Viewer, wood on pedestal
and base, 1870's . . . $45.00-60.00
Stereo Viewer, Brewster, wood,
1860's $135.00-160.00
Cine-Kodak A, Movie Camera,
1920's $125.00-150.00
Bell & Howell Model 75, Movie
Camera, 1920's $75.00-90.00

Images - All prices are for photos in excellent condition. Any defects that detract from the image also reduce the price substantially. Large size photos bring more money than similar photos of smaller size. However, due to the rise in interest of antique photography as a major collecting medium and art form, values are changing every year. These rises in values are due to various factors such as personal interests of the specific collector, size of the photograph, condition, and rarity of the specific subject matter.

Daguerreotype - 1830's-1860's
The daguerreotype, invented by Louis Daguerre in 1839, was a process in which an image was produced on a plate of copper plated with silver. It was noted for its striking clarity in detail and its mirror image. Its only difficulty was that the viewer had to turn the image at a slight angle, casting the view in a shadow, before it could be clearly seen. The Daguerreotype, being the earliest form of photography, is the rarest, and therefore, the most valuable. Basically, the values can be estimated in the following manner:
Portrait, small $7.50-50.00
Portrait, large $50.00-100.00
Portraits, famous subject $100.00+
Group portrait . . . . $125.00+
Outdoor scene . . . . $150.00+
Occupational . . . . $150.00+

Lockets, lapel pins,
brooches $50.00-150.00

Ambrotype - 1850's-1870's
The Ambrotype, invented circa 1850, was a form of photography produced directly on a glass plate. In actuality, it is a negative and the image is viewed by backing the plate with black which causes the image to appear positive. Like the Daguerreotype, it was noted for its extreme clarity in detail and did, eventually, manage to replace the Daguerreotype until the invention of the Tintype circa 1860. Ambrotypes compare favorably in value to Daguerrotypes but do not command quite as much money in like areas. The values can be estimated in the following manner:
Portrait, small $7.50-50.00
Portrait, large $35.00-100.00
Portrait, famous subject . $75.00+
Outdoor scenes . . . . $150.00+
Occupational . . . . $150.00+
Jewelry $30.00-85.00

Tintype
The tintype or Ferrotype is a direct, positive image process reproduced which gave it wide popularity between 1860 and 1910. Sizes vary from 6½" x 8½" Full Plate to the tiny 2" x 2½' ninth plate. General values pertain to specific subject matter and can be approximated in the following manner:
Portrait, small $1.00-10.00
Portrait, large $7.50-50.00
Portrait, famous subject . $75.00+
Outdoor scene . . . . $100.00+
Occupational . . . . $100.00+

Carte-de-visite
The carte-de-visite is a positive image, reproduced by a negative, on paper. The general size of the carte-de-visite is 2½' x 3¾" and it is mounted on a small, paper card

stock measuring approximately 4" x 3". The name of the photographer is usually stamped on the reverse side of the card stock. General values basically follow those of the tintype with some slightly lower figures as paper images have not reached the popularity of the earlier, so called, "hard images" as yet. Values, as for the tintype, pertain to such standards as condition, subject matter, personal interests of the specific collector, etc. However, they can be approximated in the following manner:

Portrait $1.00-2.00
Portrait, famous
   subject $10.00-70.00
Civil War $10.00-50.00

Cabinet View
The Cabinet View is a positive image, reproduced by a negative, on paper similar to the carte-de-visites. However, it is a much later process, dating primarily from the 1870's to the 1920's. The general size of the Cabinet view is approximately 4" x 5½" and it is mounted on an ornate card stock of 4¼" x 6½". This ornate card stock mounting usually bears the photographer's name and address at the bottom front of the card stock, under the actual image. Values generally follow those of the carte-de-visite and can be approximated in the following manner, following the same standards as those of the carte-de-visite and the tintype:

Portrait $1.00-2.00
Portrait, famous
   subject $7.50-50.00
Outdoor scene $7.50-50.00
Western scenes, (cowboys) $50.00+

Stereo Cards
A stereo card, when seen through the proper equipment, appears to have depth. This illusion is created by the use of side-by-side duplicate images. Though found in metal, transparent tissue and glass, paper prints on cardboard are the most common. Lithographed cards of the late 1800's are less valuable than photo cards.

Outdoor scenes $1.00-2.00
Portrait, famous
   subject $5.00-10.00
Civil War $5.00-10.00
Lithographed cards $1.00
1850's views $12.00-17.50

This lapel pin is from about 1900 and worth $20.00-30.00.

Postcards
Postcard collecting allows the collector to view past American life at its fullest. There are multitudes of categories available in which to specialize, or a random collection of many different types, styles, and periods, is also a valuable possession. Holiday postcards continue to be popular with collectors as do Lincoln, transportation, Indians, political, occupation, and Negro cards. Cards featuring the artist's signature have begun to gather a rather large following in recent years. The collector should use caution because some early cards are

These three Halloween postcards **would bring $4.00-5.00 each.**

Two early Santa Claus cards worth about $3.00 each.

being reproduced. Prices here reflect cards in good condition with no tears or defacing marks. Cards showing views and street scenes of specific locations are more valuable in their respective areas. Postcards are those with illustration on one side and space for writing on the reverse. Cards issued by the Post Office are referred to as Postal cards or postal stationery.

World War I cards	$2.00-3.00
Western life	$ .75-1.00
Street scenes	$.50-1.00
Fire departments	$2.50-4.00
Comic cards	$ .50-1.00
Automobile advertising	$5.00-15.00
Ships	$1.50-2.50
Lindbergh	$4.00-7.00
Political cards	$5.00-20.00
Nudes, pinups	$3.00-6.50
Christmas, Santa Claus	$ .50-3.00
Halloween	$3.50-6.00
July Fourth	$3.00-7.00
Easter	$ .75-2.00
Birthday	$ .50-1.50
Disaster	$1.50-2.50

Pocket Knives

Pocket knives are extremely popular trade items. Thousands of knives have been manufactured over the years, making it possible for many collectors and enthusiasts to actively participate in collecting knives. Case knives are one of the most popular brands but Remington, Winchester and others are close behind. Prices

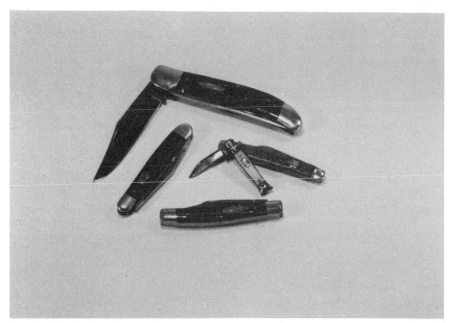

A selection of pocket knives.

here are for used knives, sharpened, but still in excellent condition, with no blade nicks or other surface defects. Mint knives would be worth about twice as much.

Case Muskrat, "Hawbaker's
  Special," bone stag
  handles $15.00-18.00
Winchester, 1920, single blade,
  bone handles $100.00
Remington, R4353, two blade,
  stag handles .... $100.00 +
Case, 53047, three blade, stag
  handle $25.00-30.00
Case, 3201, two blade .. $4.50-7.50
Case, 62009, two blade . $3.50-5.00
Case, 6227, two blade .. $4.50-8.00
Case, 8261, two blade . $7.50-10.00
Case, 06263FSS, two
  blade $7.50-10.00
Case, Whittler, three
  blade $9.00-12.00
Case, 13031LR
  Electrician $8.00-10.00
Case, 33092, Birds eye,
  3 blade $12.00-15.00

Case, 6488, 4 blade ... $12.00-15.00
Cattaraugus, 20228 .. $12.00-15.00
Cattaraugus, 23669-N $10.00-15.00
Cattaraugus, 35151 .. $30.00-40.00
Remington, R2 ...... $15.00-17.00
Remington, RC6 .... $15.00-17.00
Remington, R325 .... $35.00-37.50
Winchester, 2207 .... $70.00-85.00
Winchester, 2924 .... $45.00-50.00
Albertson Co. $20.00-25.00
Adams & Son $7.50-8.00
American Ace $22.50-25.00
Banner Cutlery Co. .. $12.00-15.00
Boker, Solingen,
  Germany $10.00-12.00
Browning, No. 3018 .. $20.00-25.00

Primitives

Primitives are pieces, usually hand made, that were used by pioneers 100 years ago or more. These primitives are becoming more popular as decorating accessories. Because they were generally made by hand, there is the chance that any two examples of a certain item could differ slightly. At the present time, their value is increasing but they still remain reasonably inexpensive in many cases. The collector should be very careful when buying primitives because some items are being reproduced.

Sugar bucket, wood, original
   paint $75.00-90.00
Bee smoker $35.00-45.00
Salt box, lidded,
   hanging $20.00-25.00
Corn husking peg, wood and
   leather $5.00-10.00
Spoon rack with
   drawers $75.00-100.00
Soft soap scoop $75.00-100.00
Wash dolly, 37'',
   wood $30.00-40.00
Tinder box, tin with steel and
   flint . . . . $200.00 +
Pully, wood, carved . . . $8.00-12.00
Rope bed key, wood . . $25.00-30.00
Garden reel, wood and
   string $125.00-150.00
Spinning wheel, small,
   wood . . . . $225.00 +
Click reel, wood $90.00-110.00
Grape press, wood, pegged
   construction $70.00-80.00

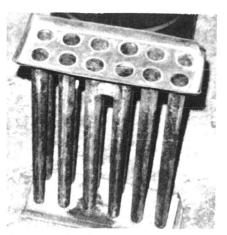

A metal 12-stick candle mold, mid 1800's. $75.00.

This wooden washboard is from the 1840's. $75.00 +.

Apple dryer, cherry and
   wire $30.00-35.00
Rope jack, wood,
   1780 . . . . $35.00-40.00
Birch broom, 1800's . . . $8.00-10.00
Candle snuffer, tin . . . $20.00-25.00
Flour scoop, wood,
   1850's $12.00-17.50

Maple mortar and pestle, 1700's. $200.00

The cherry dough raiser is worth about $50.00. The dough rollers are valued at $25.00-35.00.

Quilts

Quilts and needlework have gained new popularity in recent years. The presence of hand prepared work makes the quilt, sampler or rug an item that takes many hours of skilled watchful labor. The value depends on several factors. First, and foremost, is the quality of work and details that have been included. Also important is the quality of material and the condition of the piece. Cross stitched coverings are generally more valuable than pieced quilts.

A signed alphabet sampler, $125.00-160.00

Sampler, 1860's, alphabet,
  signed . . . . $200.00 +
Rug, applique,
  coin spot $75.00-100.00
Quilt, Log Cabin . . $120.00-150.00
Quilt, signature $125.00-150.00

Quilt, homespun,
  patchwork $65.00-75.00
Quilt, Tree of Life . . . . . $200.00 +
Quilt, Lily of the
  Field $125.00-150.00
Quilt, Flying Geese . $130.00-160.00

Quilts. At top left is the Tree of Life pattern; at top right a geometric design. Bottom left is the Double Wedding Ring pattern; bottom right is Grandma's Flower Garden.

Sampler, 1840's, linen, alphabet
   & illustration $150.00-300.00
Doilies, crocheted $1.00-5.00

Railroad Collectibles
Anything that was actually used by a railroad or anything picturing trains is considered to be a railroad collectible. Stamps, postcards, timetables, signs, lanterns, glassware, locks, water and oilcans, badges, uniforms, are all in demand from collectors of train memorabilia. Stocks, bonds, photographs and advertising material are also very popular.

Long snout oil can, Missouri
   Pacific $30.00-35.00
Uniform button, Alton, gold,
   flat $2.00-3.00
Calendar, 1957, Santa
   Fe $9.00-11.00
Calendar, 1927, Centennial,
   B&O $25.00-30.00

Kerosene can, UPRR,
embossed $15.00-20.00
Cap badge, Boston & Maine
Trainman, nickel . . $20.00-25.00
Dinner plate, 1927 Centennial,
B&O $30.00-35.00
Dinner plate, C & NW, Shenango
China $70.00-75.00
Silver flatware teaspoon, ICRR,
Reed & Barton $7.00-10.00
Silver flatware dinner knife, Rock
Island $12.00-15.00
Shot glass, Union
Pacific $4.00-5.00
Tumbler, frosted, D&H . $6.00-7.50
Caboose lamp, Safety Co., 1900's,
brass $40.00-50.00

Vacation folder map, Burlington
Route Yellowstone . . . $5.00-7.50

Cuspidor, Pullman,
nickel $50.00-60.00

Telegraph key, GN,
1880's $45.00-55.00

Ticket, 500 miles, CV,
1880's $5.00-7.00
Timetables, Alton, 1932 $6.00-8.00
Timetables, Burlington Route,
1930's $6.00-8.00
Track Shovel, CB & Q $16.00-18.00
Pipe wrench, NYC . . . $12.00-15.00
Watch for Northern
Pacific $12.00-15.00
Broom, C & NW $10.00-12.00
Door handle, L & N,
brass $35.00-45.00
Footstool, Great
Northern $90.00-100.00
Mail pouch, Railway
Express $35.00-40.00
Coal shovel, AT & SF $20.00-25.00
Playing cards, B & O,
1920's $15.00-20.00
Pinback button, C & O,
Chessie Cat $12.00-15.00
Passenger pass, Chicago &
Northwestern
1890's $10.00-12.00

New York Central fire bucket,
$20.00-$30.00; Wabash bucket,
$12.00-$15.00.

Kerosene railroad hand lantern, Nashville to Franklin, $75.00. from a defunct line that ran from

Carbide Railroad lantern, $25.00; spikes, 50¢-$1.00.

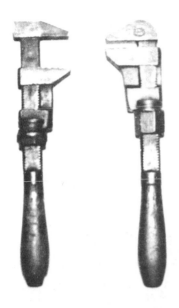

These railroad wrenches from Illinois Central and Baltimore and Ohio are worth about $40.00 each.

Razors

In the 19th Century competition was great among the steel producers in the United States, England and Germany to produce the most popular and best razor. There are, as a result, many types of razors and also many materials used to form the handles. Whale bone, ivory, composition, clay, and gold are a few of the materials that were popular with the razor makers. Colelctible razors are those free from rust and corrosion. Broken blades, gaps, and nicks reduce the price of a razor considerably. The handle must also be in excellent condition, regardless of the material used. Markings appear on the blade and tang of the razor rather than the handle. To use these listings add the value of the manufacturer to the value of the handle material.

Blade Manufacturers

Abrams & Son	$1.00
American Knife Co.	$3.00-7.00
E. Barnard	$10.00-12.00
Belknap	$1.00-2.00
W.R. Case & Sons	$8.00-12.00
Cattaragus Cutlery	$5.00-6.00
Elgin	$1.00-2.00
B.S. Eyre	$3.00-5.00
Franklin Cutlery	$1.00-2.00
Gilbert Bros.	$3.00-4.00
Groesbreck & Co.	$5.00-10.00
Henry Harrington	$8.00-17.00
Hollinger	$1.00-2.00
Jones Mfg.	$1.00-2.00
Albert Jordan	$3.00-4.00
August Kern	$1.00-3.00
J.C.X. Land	$7.00-8.50
W.H. Morley & Sons	$2.00-4.00

A razor showing the areas used to mark the manufacturers name or trademark.

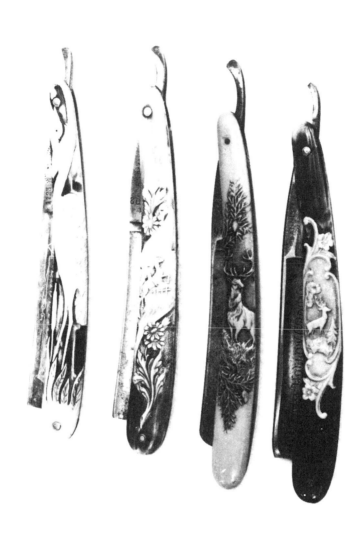

Four ornate celluloid handled razors.

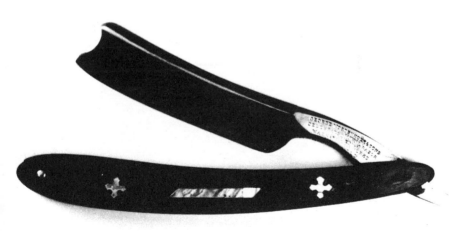

Top: 1840 bone handle razor; bottom: 1850's horn handle razor.

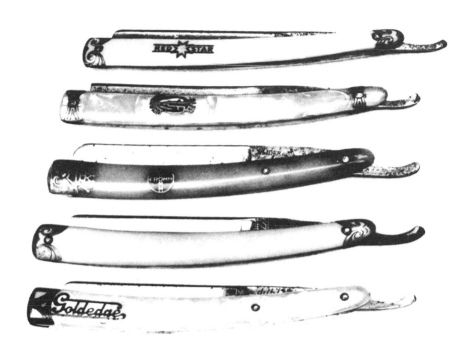

A selection of straight razors with fancy ends from Germany.

New England Cutlery	$1.00-2.00
Norvill & Kippox	$3.00-6.00
Parker & Linley	$6.00-10.00
John Primble	$2.00-3.00
I. Rosenbaum	$1.00-2.00
Slater Brothers	$7.00-13.00
Thomas Turner & Co.	$5.00-7.00
Union & Rodgers	$12.00-15.00
Walker & Gibson	$2.00-3.00
John Wragg	$8.00-9.00

Handles. Prices are for plain handles.

Black horn, before 1850	$7.00-15.00
Black horn, after 1850	$2.00-5.00
Clear horn, before 1850	$10.00-20.00
Clear horn, after 1850	$10.00-20.00
Bone, before 1850	$10.00-20.00
Bone, after 1850	$5.00-7.00

Sterling	$55.00+
Silverplate	$10.00-25.00
Aluminum	$5.00-15.00

Rockwell Collectibles

Norman Rockwell was probably the most popular and well known American artist and illustrator of all time. His illustrations decorated the covers of *The Saturday Evening Post* for nearly half a century. Rockwell art can be seen in advertising from Coca-Cola to Ford Motor Company to Schmidts with a multitude of products in between. Rockwell art in its original use as well as figurines, plates, prints, or other reproductions are considered collectible. Keep in mind that many Rockwell products are still being manufactured.

Postcard, Baseball Hall of Fame,
1950's $5.00-7.50
Box, Kellogg's Cornflakes,
1950's, 5 types each $17.50-22.50
Fan, Boy Scouts of
America $25.00-27.00
Poster, A T & T, 1976 reprint of
early ad featuring
lineman $5.00-7.50
Blotter, Edison Mazda Lamps,
1920's $25.00
Display poster, Schmidts' Beer,
1930's card game . . $60.00-65.00
"Boy Scout Handbook",
1940 . . . . $10.00-12.00
Santa Claus cardboard cut out,
Pepsi, 2' tall $50.00
Sheet music, "Over
There" $35.00-50.00
Ads, single page, clipped from
magazine . . . . . . each $2.00-5.00

Saturday Evening Post, covers,
1916 . . . . $20.00-50.00
Saturday Evening Post, covers,
1917-1926 . . . . each $15.00-25.00
Saturday Evening Post, covers,
1927-1936 . . . . each $10.00-22.00
Saturday Evening Post, covers,
1937-1946 . . . . . each $5.00-17.50
Saturday Evening Post, covers,
1947-1963 . . . . . each $5.00-12.00
Tray, Coca-Cola, "Tom
Sawyer", 1930's . $125.00-175.00
Plates, set of 4, Gorham China
1972, "Young Love, 4
Seasons" $95.00-115.00
Ink blotter, Coca-Cola, "Tom
Sawyer, 1930's $45.00-50.00
Plastic coin, Ford 50 year
anniversary, 1950's $10.00-12.00
Norman Rockwell autograph, sign-
ed letter, 1920's . . $175.00-200.00

This Norman Rockwell *Saturday* **worth $7.00-10.00.**
Evening Post **cover from 1960 is**

Red Wing Stoneware. Top Row: Spongeware bowl, $35.00; stone jar, $20.00. Second row: Jug, $20.00; bird feeder, $35.00. Bottom row: 2 gallon crocks, $25.00 each.

Red Wing Pottery

Red Wing Pottery from Minnesota, like other defunct potteries, is being collected across the country. Red Wing made dinnerware, crockery, cookie jars, and other practical as well as decorative pieces.

Roseville Pottery

Roseville pottery was first made in

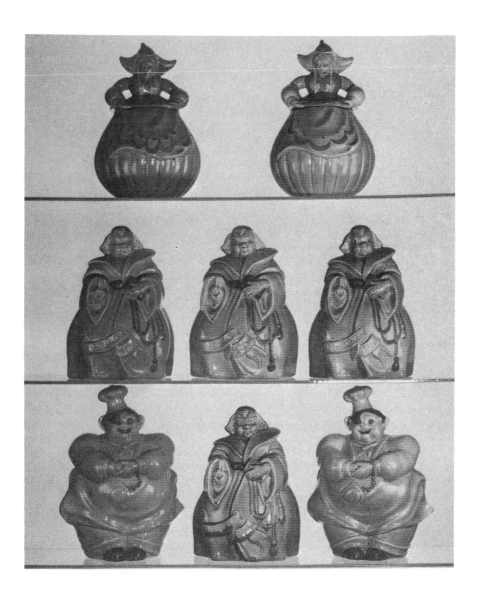

A group of Red Wing cookie jars, **$25.00-30.00 each.**

of the potters was artist signed, hand painted pottery. This artist signed pottery is by far the most valuable today. Many other types of pottery were produced, both marked and unmarked, and all types are popular with collectors. The collector should be careful not to confuse the hand painted pottery with the pieces that have been decorated with transfer designs.

Chocolate pot, Creamware,
  10" .... $225.00+
Dresser set, Forget Me
  Not .... $225.00+
Vase, 6", Carnelian .. $20.00-25.00
Urn, 8" Carnelian ... $35.00-45.00
Basket, 6", Imperial I $40.00-45.00
Flower pot & saucer,
  Donatello $40.00-50.00
Double bud vase, Donatello,
  5" $30.00-35.00

Roseville Rozane art pottery. Top row: 9″ vase $165.00-$225.00; bud vase $75.00-$90.00; urn $175.00-$225.00. Bottom row: bowl, $125.00-$175.00; vase $100-$150.00.

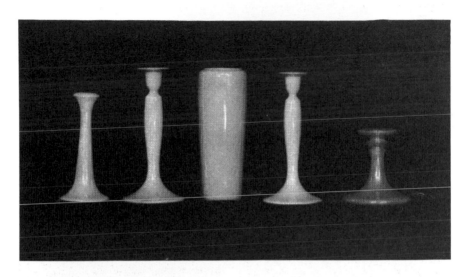

Roseville Lustre candleholders and vases from the 1920's. Each is worth **$35.00-65.00.**

Console bowl, Tuscany,
   11" $35.00-40.00
Lamp, Florentine $75.00-85.00
Vase, Cremona, 8" .. $40.00-45.00
Jardiniere,
   Sunflower $80.00-100.00
Cornucopia vase,
   Thornapple $25.00-30.00

Vase, Clemana, 7" ... $80.00-90.00
Vase, 6", Earlam $50.00-60.00
Bud vase, 6", Futura . $35.00-40.00
Candleholder, 4½",
   Moss $40.00-45.00
Basket, Cosmos, 12" . $75.00-85.00
Wall pocket, Blackberry $150.00 +
Bowl, Jonquil, 4" ... $45.00-50.00

These two pieces of Roseville pottery are from the Imperial II pattern. The vase on the left is valued at **$40.00-55.00, and the wall pocket on the right is worth about $75.00--85.00.**

Jug base, 7",
   Cherry Blossom . $100.00-125.00
Console bowl, 12",
   Wisteria $75.00-85.00
Vase, 8", Laurel $40.00-45.00
Bowl, 4" Luffa $35.00-40.00
Vase, 9½" Topeo . $125.00-150.00
Bowl, 6" Orian $60.00-70.00
Double bud vase, 8"
   Velmoss $45.00-50.00
Urn vase, 6" Morning
   Glory $100.00-125.00
Basket, 10", Teasel . . $65.00-75.00

Salt Shakers

Salt shaker collecting was once considered merely a sideline to serious glassware collectors, the majority of quality salt shakers being included in collections because of the pattern. Salt shakers have become popular in recent years in their own right. Art and pattern glass salt shakers wee made in many patterns and styles, and there are hundreds available to collectors. The collector should be cautious in buying salt shakers, because some reproductions are available.

Star of Bethlehem, Cambridge,
   1910 . . . . $25.00-30.00
Cotton bale, aqua,
   1890's $30.00-35.00
Heart, pink, 1890's . . $35.00-40.00
Spider web, blue,
   1890's $30.00-40.00

A Scroll Wave salt shaker from the late 1890's, valued at $70.00-80.00.

Acorn, 1880's, white . $35.00-50.00
Sphinx, 1920, clear . . . $60.00-70.00
Iris, 1905, green $25.00-30.00
Ribbed Thumbprint,
  ruby & clear $15.00-20.00
Dice, with painted flowers, 1890,
  custard $85.00-100.00
Crown Milano, 1895, painted
  flowers $100.00-125.00
Fig, 1890, custard . . $100.00-125.00
Bird Arbor, 1880's, hand painted
  bird & floral $100.00-115.00
Cornucopia, 1930's,
  clear $30.00-35.00
Cabin in the Snow, 1890's
  hand painted $100.00-125.00
Beaded Heart, 1900,
  custard $25.00-40.00

Schoenhut Dolls and Toys

The wooden dolls and toys of the A. Schoenhut Company are demanding premium prices today from both doll and toy collectors. First produced around the turn of the Century, the Humpty Dumpty Circus is probably the most popular of the Schoenhut products. This collection of animals, acrobats, clowns, ringmaster, lion tamers, and other circus figures and equipment can bring over $125.00 or more for each in good condition. Production of dolls began shortly before World War I, and these lifelike wood dolls are very popular among collectors. Also produced by Schoenhut were

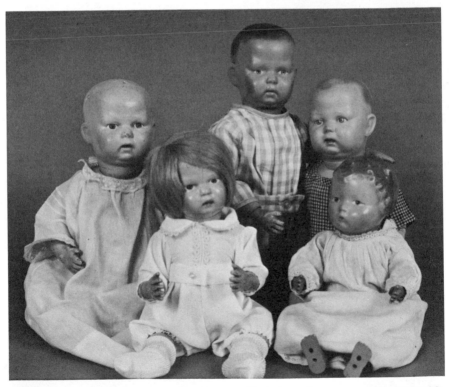

This group of wood dolls by Schoenhut contains babys with bent limbs in the 13" and 15" sizes. A Schoenhut doll of this type and style will bring from around $250.00-350.00. The small doll in the right corner has a wood "composition" head.

This 18″ girl is valued at $300.00. The "Felix the Cat" figure $100.00.

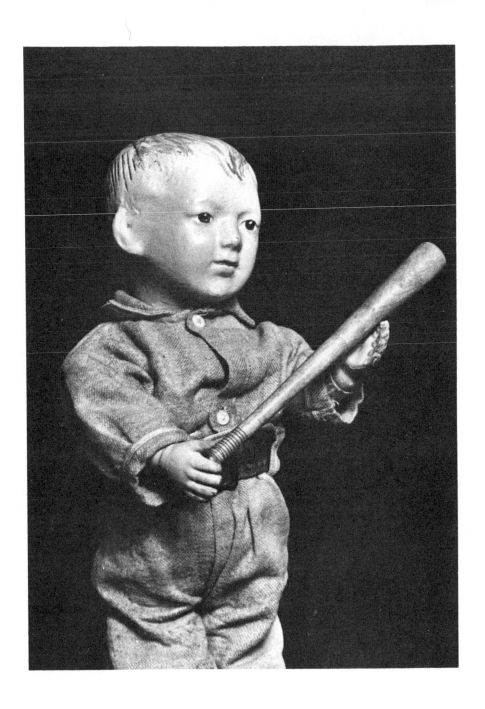

A 16″ boy in a baseball suit with carved hair is worth $650.00 or more.

character figures, puppets, doll houses and furniture, pianos and other excellent quality toys for both boys and girls.

Dolls

Baby doll, wood head, cloth body,
with voice box . . . . $300.00 +
Boy and Girl, twins,
16" . . . . $1000.00 +
Boy, 17", 4 teeth . . . . . . $225.00 +
Girl, 14" walker . . . . $350.00 +
Girl, 16" closed mouth . . $225.00 +
Salesman sample cut away to show
construction . . . . $800.00 +
Girl, 22", in sailor suit . . $375.00 +

Figures & Circus People
(approximately 8" in height)
Chinaman . . . . $125.00 +

African drummer . . . . . . $300.00 +
Clown, silk suit . . . . $100.00 +
Clown, cotton suit . . . . $100.00 +
Farmer . . . . $200.00 +
Gent Acrobat . . . . $175.00 +
Lady bareback rider . . . . $175.00 +
Milk Wagon driver . . . . . $150.00 +
Teddy Roosevelt . . . . $450.00 +

Animals
Alligator, glass eyes . . . . $125.00 +
Buffalo, cloth ruff,
glass eyes . . . . $125.00 +
Camel, (one hump) . . . . . $175.00 +
Camel, (two humps) . . . . $175.00 +
Gorilla . . . . $300.00 +
Kangaroo . . . . $350.00 +
Monkey . . . . $175.00 +
Tiger . . . . $125.00 +
Zebra . . . . $125.00 +

A group of circus performers and animals from Schoenhut's Menagerie set. Any of the figures in this photo will bring well over **$125.00. This is one of the many sets of groupings of circus figures sold by Schoenhut.**

Shaker Collectibles

The Shakers or United Society of Believers in Christ's Second Appearing were a very simplistic religious cult that made beautiful, yet simple furnishings and tools. The furniture is without decorative accessories and is utilitarian in design. Because this furniture was of good solid construction and the group is no longer in existence, values for Shaker furniture and crafts are high. Beware of reproduction Shaker furniture and modern furniture in the Shaker style.

Child's rocker with arms,
    tape seat . . . . $350.00 +

Ladderback rocker, woven rush
    seat $200.00
Ladderback side chair, reed
    seat $250.00
Sewing basket, 4
    pockets $100.00-125.00
Foot stool, (signed) $150.00-175.00
Spice box, oval $85.00-100.00
Cheese basket . . . . $250.00 +
Apple parer, wood . . . . . $175.00 +
Cheese form $50.00
Grain measure, covered,
    signed $125.00
Pantry boxes, wood, oval,
    painted, set of 3 . . . . $170.00
Yarn Swift, maple . $160.00-175.00
Seed box with label . . . . . $200.00 +
Ladderback straight chair with
    arms, rush seat . . $250.00-325.00
Cloak hanger $130.00-140.00

Shaker "production" chairs from Mt. Lebanon, New York. Each of these rockers is worth $700.00 or more.

237

This "fancy" Shaker basket is from the turn of the century.

Shawnee Pottery

Shawnee pottery was made in Ohio from 1937 until 1961. The inexpensive products of the company were sold primarily through cabin and department stores. Since the closing of the pottery works in 1961, the pieces have become more popular with collectors. The most familiar pieces of Shawnee pottery are the cookie jars and the very popular "corn" pieces, made to resemble ears of corn. The salt and pepper sets of smiling pigs and sailors are also popular.

Cookie Jars

Figural Dutch girl	$20.00-25.00
Figural Dutch boy . . .	$20.00-25.00
Farmer Pig	$25.00-30.00
Puss in Boots	$25.00-30.00
Smiley Pig	$25.00-35.00
Winnie Pig	$25.00-35.00

Mugsey Dog	$25.00-30.00
Owl	$25.00-30.00
Basket of Fruit	$20.00-25.00

Corn items

Cookie jar	$25.00-30.00
Teapot	$20.00-25.00
Milk pitcher	$15.00-20.00
Mixing bowl	$7.50-10.00
Covered casserole	$9.00-11.00
Platter	$12.00-15.00
Salt & pepper, large . .	$11.00-13.00
Salt & pepper, small . . .	$8.00-10.00
Relish tray	$5.00-8.00

Salt & Peppers

Milk pails	$7.50-10.00
Standing elephants	$7.50-10.00
Mugsey Dog	$10.00-12.00
Owl	$10.00-12.00
Little Bo Peep	$11.00-13.00
Sailor Boy	$10.00-12.00

A group of Shawnee cookie jars   worth from $20.00-35.00.

A group of the popular "corn" pieces of Shawnee Pottery.

Shawnee salt & pepper shakers.

Sheet Music

Popularity of sheet music peaked during the "Tin Pan Alley Days," from the 1880's until the 1930's. There was fierce competition between song publishers and the graphics used to adorn the covers of the sheets are indeed works of art. Millions of pieces of sheet music were engulfed by an eager public wanting to play and sing the sad songs of the '90's, patriotic songs of the war years, and the happy silly or romantic songs of the times in between. Most pieces are still priced low enough to allow many more collectors into the field.

Ballin' the Jack,
  1900's $10.00-12.00
Cabin in the Sky,
  1940's $1.00-2.00
Down in the Subway,
  1900's $5.00-7.00
Five Minutes More,
  1940's $1.00-2.00
Going My Way, 1940's . $1.00-2.00
Hawaiian Butterfly,
  1900's $2.00-5.00
Hold Me, 1920's $3.00-4.00
I Have Eyes, 1920's $3.00-5.00
Jealous, 1920's $2.00-3.50
Just Like A Rainbow,
  1920's $2.00-3.00
Laughing Irish Eyes,
  1930's $3.00-5.00
Marie, 1920's $2.00-4.00

Calico Rag, $5.00-$7.00.

Sheet music, The Big Brown Bear, 1919 is valued at $2.00-3.00. Music **from the Jolson Story, 1940's would bring about $3.00.**

242

Nobody Lied, 1920's ... $3.00-4.00
Old South, late
  1800's $10.00-15.00
Over There, 1900's ... $20.00-30.00
Paper Doll, 1900's $2.00-4.00
Red Moon, 1920's $2.00-4.00
Should I, 1920's $3.00-5.00
Ting-A-Ling, 1930's $1.00-2.00
Uncle Sammy, 1900's ... $3.00-4.00
Victory, 1900's $2.00-3.00
What'll I Do, 1920's $3.00-5.00
Yankee Doodle, 1940's . $1.00-2.00
You Hit The Spot,
  1930's $2.00-4.00

Shirley Temple Collectibles

Shirley Temple, the dimpled little actress of the thirties, was one of the most popular performers of the day. In 1934, Ideal's first Shirley Temple doll began a flood of toys, dolls, books, cards, pins, records and games that was immediately as popular as the cute little girl. The charm of Shirley Temple is still evident today as collectors pay premium prices for the memorabilia that is related in any way. The collector should be cautious in buying Shirley Temple items because some are being reproduced. Dolls in special clothes are worth considerably more.

Composition Dolls, mint in original clothes, with original hair set.
7½" $75.00
11" $175.00
13" $130.00
15" or 16" $145.00
17" or 18" $165.00
19" or 20" $185.00
21" or 22" $200.00
23" or 24" $250.00
25" $300.00

"Goodnight My Love" from the Shirley Temple movie "Stowaway".

Shirley Temple sheet music usually brings from $12.00-20.00.

Vinyl (mint in original clothes with original hair set).
12" $45.00
15" $65.00
17" $85.00
Fountain pen, 1930's $20.00
Trade cards, 1930's $5.00
Postcards, 1930's,
    1940's $2.00-5.00
Big Little Books, 1930's $10.00
Heidi, (book) 1937,
    Saalfield $15.00

I Am Eight, (book) 1937,
    Saalfield $15.00
Bowl, General Mills, blue with
    white photo $25.00
Plastic tea set, 1950's, pink,
    in box $30.00
Doll Buggy, wood $75.00
Coloring book, "Bluebird", 1930's,
    Saalfield $20.00
Coloring and Paperdoll book,
    "Birthday Book", Saalfield,
    1935 .... $35.00

This sound track from some early Shirley Temple movies was released in the 1950's, and is worth about $10.00-15.00.

Cereal Pitcher given away by General Mills. $25.00. A bowl and smaller pitcher were also available.

Simon & Halbig 19'' character, $350.00-400.00.

This large, 36'' Simon and Halbig is valued at $500.00-600.00.

Simon & Halbig Dolls

Simon & Halbig manufactured dolls from the latter part of the 19th centuries until the 1930's. It became one of the largest German firms and made heads for many French doll makers in the 1870's and 1880's. Many of the Simon & Halbig dolls had moveable eyes. Like other German dolls of the period these high quality dolls have high price tags.

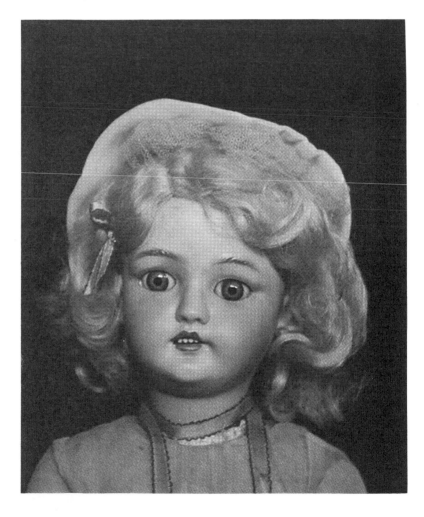

A 25" Simon & Halbig doll, $200.00-300.00.

21" socket head, composition body, sleep eyes, open mouth $175.00 +

18" socket head, composition body, closed mouth .... $450.00 +

25" socket head, composition body, set eyes, closed mouth $600.00 +

8" shoulder head, cloth body, closed mouth, sleep eyes .... $225.00 +

19½" shoulder head, open mouth, paperweight set eyes, pierced ears .... $200.00 +

16" brown bisque socket head, sleep eyes, open mouth, Hindu .... $450.00 +

32" socket head, composition body, set eyes, open mouth .. $300.00 +

10" socket head, composition body, sleep eyes, open mouth $125.00-175.00

29" shoulder head, muslin body, bisque arms, open mouth $300.00 +

18" turned shoulder head, open mouth .... $200.00 +

13" socket head, sleep almond shaped eyes, olive skin .... $700.00 +

25" socket head, adult composition body, open mouth, pierced ears .... $500.00 +

24" shoulder head, open mouth, bisque arms, kid body $250.00 +

15½" socket head, wood & composition body, pierced ears, open mouth .... $800.00 +

25" socket head, spring strung body, modeled eyebrows, pierced ears, set eyes, open mouth .... $200.00 +

29" socket head, composition body, sleep eyes, open mouth, pierced ears, modeled eyebrows .... $250.00 +

16½" socket head, composition body, sleep eyes, pierced ears .... $150.00 +

19" socket head, toddler body, flirty sleep eyes, open mouth, upper teeth & tongue . $300.00 +

A Winchester cartridge board from the 1890's. $1000.00 +

249

A carbide burning lamp and tin for storing carbide. $25.00-50.00.

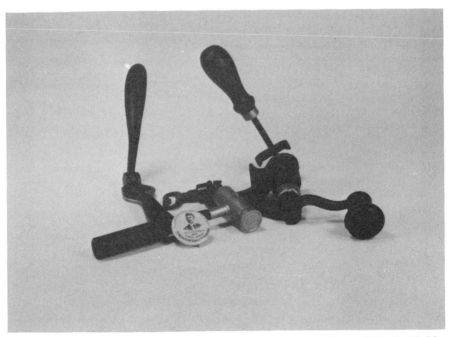

Hunting and gun related material are eagerly sought. The Winchester pinback featuring sharpshooter Adolph Topperwein from the early 1900's is valued at $10.00-20.00. The complete set of early reloading tools is worth $35.00-75.00.

Compasses are good sporting collectibles. The compass on the left in a wood case with brass fittings is from the late 1800's and will bring $25.00-30.00. The brass compass on the right is from the early 1900's and is worth about $10.00-20.00.

Casting reel, Pennell, Kentucky
style, 1920's $35.00-50.00
Fly reel, Pfleuger, Golden West
early 1900's $125.00-175.00
Sextant, brass, early
1900's. $225.00-250.00
Field glasses, 1890's, black leather
case $25.00-50.00
Ice Skates, wood with iron blade
and heel cup, 1870's $25.00-50.00
Riding crop, stag and silver handle
leather, 1890's. . . $100.00-115.00
Calendar, Harrington &
Richardson, 1907 . . . . $250.00+
Calendar, Union Metalic Cartridge
Co., 1902 . . . . $200.00+
Poster, Peters, 1909, men
in canoe . . . . $200.00+
Stereo cards, lithographed, hunting
scenes, late 1800's. . . . $1.00-2.00

Sporting Collectibles
Hunting and fishing paraphernalia head the list of popular sporting collectibles but collectibles of yachting, boating, horse racing and riding, boxing, bicycling, etc., are steadily gaining ground. Just about anything remotely related to the activities are considered collectible including paintings, stamps, and figures as well as actual equipment.

Stained Glass
Stained glass has reached new popularity in recent years with good examples bringing several hundred dollars or more. Stained glass windows and lamps are made with pieces of colored glass molded together or actual painted glass. The windows are especially popular in house restoring or remodeling. Signed examples bring premium prices.

An advertising stained glass window worth about $600.00 or more.

Stained glass lamp shades are both beautiful and expensive. Each of these would cost around $1000.00.

Stock Certificates

Stock and bond collecting or "Scripophily" has only recently become popular with collectors. Most collectible stocks are no longer negotiable and factors influencing value are the type company issuing the stock, how pleasing to the eye the certificate is, signatures on the certificates, and condition. Prices here are for cancelled stocks.

American Express, 1850's, signed by H. Wells & W. Fargo .... $850.00+

Canadian Edison Phonograph, Ltd., 1920's, signed by T. Edison .... $525.00+

International Nickel Co., 1912 .... $5.00

Houdini Picture Corporation, 1920's, signed by H. Houdini .... $650.00+

Alabama Gold and Copper Mining Co., 1899, signed by Pat Garrett $100.00-115.00

Carolina Savings Bank, 1870's $15.00-20.00

Pierre Arrow Motor Car Co., 1917 .... $25.00-30.00

Northampton Brewery Corp., 1930's $5.00-6.00

Sanitary Paper Milk Bottle Co., 1907 .... $10.00-12.00

Acme Uranium Mines Co., 1950's $1.00-2.50

San Luis Valley Irrigation, 1905 .... $5.00-7.00

Island Creek Coal Co., 1930's $3.00-5.00

Missouri, Kansas and Texas Railway, 1900 .... $12.00-15.00

Chicago and North Western Railway, 1940's $2.00-3.00

Standard Oil, late 1800's, John D. Rockefeller signature .... $750.00+

A stock certificate from the Missouri, Kansas, Texas Railroad Company valued at about $5.00-10.00. Earlier certificates from the same railroad are worth a few dollars more.

253

Two popular wall phones from the early 1900's in oak cases. Each is worth about $150.00 or more.

Telephones

Telephones have evolved over the years making the old wall and candlestick style phones very popular with collectors. There are several different makes and styles of phones on the market today but probably most popular is the oak wall phone manufactured around the turn of the century. Even cradle phones from the 1930's and 1940's are being bought by collectors, as are old switchboards and other memorabilia. Use caution when buying old telephones because reproductions are available.

Desk type, candlestick, brass,
  early 1900's . . . . $100.00 +
Desk type, candlestick,
  1920's $50.00-75.00
Wall type, late 1800's
  oak case $130.00-180.00

Wall type, early 1900's,
  walnut case $140.00-185.00
French, cradle . . . . $100.00 +
Desk type, candlestick with dial,
  1930's $35.00-45.00
Desk type, 1930's $25.00-30.00
Bell box $25.00-30.00
Danish dial phone . . . $30.00-40.00
Dutch, cradle with ivory
  mouthpiece $45.00-60.00
Pay phone, 1920's . . . $25.00-50.00
Pay phone, 1940's . . . $20.00-25.00

Tins

Tins, containers that contained products, were used to keep contents fresh. Some have paper labels but many are lithographed onto the container. These are generally colorful attractive containers and a wide variety is available. Be careful to avoid reissued tins and reproductions of old popular tins.

Chase & Sanborn Coffee sample tin. This small, 2"x2½" tin is worth about $15.00.

Green Turtle Cigars,
  lunch box . . . . $150.00 +
Henderson & Sons, biscuits
  cabin shape $80.00-95.00
Atlantic & Pacific Tea Co. (A&P)
  old woman $75.00-85.00
White Bear Coffee,
  polar bear $15.00-20.00
Kings Herold Cigars . . . . $300.00 +
Pepper's Ace, tin & glass counter
  display, biplane . . . $75.00-85.00

A Colgate Baby Talc tin, $30.00.

Lucky Strike, pocket
  tin $20.00-25.00
Bambino, tobacco, pocket
  tin . . . . Rare
Hodgins Honey,
  cylinder $18.00-25.00
P.C.W. Cough Drops,
  small $18.00-25.00
San Blas Coconut,
  jungle scene $40.00-50.00
Toyland Peanut Butter, pail,
  band scene $45.00-50.00
Wonderful Dream Salve, small,
  round $5.00-7.50
Puritan Spices, paper
  label $65.00-75.00

Toddy Chocolate-this tin will bring $10.00-$12.00.

Huylers Pepsin Gum, paper label,
  heart shape $25.00-35.00
Sweet-Heart Sugar cones,
  cylinder $65.00-75.00
Lady Hellen Coffee,
  cylinder $20.00-30.00
Towles Log Cabin, cabin shape,
  bear in door $65.00-75.00
Towles Log Cabin, cabin on
  wheels $85.00-95.00
Navy Tobacco, small,
  sailor $25.00-35.00

These awls are worth about $3.00-5.00 each, the brass oil can $15.00-20.00.

Coopers pull scraper, $20.00-25.00.

Tools

As mechanized labor became more practical in this country, the use of the hand tool sharply declined. Improvements in design and styling also contributed to the replacement of early hand tools with more modern versions. Collectors of antique tools generally use the items for decoration rather than actual work. The prices here are for original tools with no new parts or pieces. Evidence that the tool has been used in years past adds to the over-all appeal of the piece, and a used tool is generally more in demand than a mint version.

Buzzard's wing broadaxe, $75.00.

Broad axe, goosewing, 17th
century . . . . $350.00 +
Log tongs $35.00-40.00
Carpenter's adze $50.00-60.00
Carriage ironers, double faced
hammer $22.50-30.00
Smith's punch $15.00-20.00
Button tongs $15.00-20.00
Blacksmith pincers $5.00-15.00
Burn auger $25.00-30.00
Bench drill $45.00-50.00
Hacksaw, iron, wood
handle $35.00-45.00
Shoeing stand $25.00-30.00
Hoof knives $15.00-25.00
Hoof scraper $8.00-10.00
Hoof rasp $10.00-12.00
Wheelwright's mallet . $15.00-20.00
Bricklayer's hammer . $12.00-15.00
Slater's pick $25.00-30.00
Broadaxe, buzzard
wing $75.00-100.00
Glut, oak, iron
band $10.00-12.00
Peeling chisel $55.00-65.00
Barking spud $55.00-65.00
Chain tongs $35.00-45.00
Log roller $10.00-15.00

Spiral auger $40.00-50.00
Tanner's stretching
board $15.00-20.00
Tinner's anvil $45.00-55.00
Tongue and groove
planes $50.00-60.00
Frame saw $35.00-40.00
Drawknife $20.00-30.00
Calipers, iron and
brass $27.00-35.00

Toys

Toys are very desirable collectors items. Most popular are the cast iron and tin toys, but those made of wood, glass, paper and celluloid are also very wise choices for the collector. To be collectible, toys must be in good condition with no missing pieces or parts and mechanical toys must be in working order. Toys fashioned after popular characters are highly prized collectibles. Military toys, animals, and vehicles make up a large portion of available toys but these are still good pieces. The collector should beware of reproduction toys.

These lithographed tin rooms are from Marx "Home Town". With original accessories they will bring about $25.00-35.00 each. Add $5.00 if they are still in original boxes.

The "Old Woman in the Shoe". The bisque old woman and her five children with original clothes and shoe home should bring $125.00 or more. The children's story book "The Christmas Box" is worth about $7.00-$10.00.

258

Washing machine, tin,
1940's $3.00-5.00

Top, wood, with string,
1930's $3.00-5.00

Pull toy, jockey on large dog,
tin . . . . $300.00 +

Drum, 1920's $8.00-10.00

Airplane, "Lindy" type, Barclay,
1930's $2.00-4.00

Windup band, Marx Merry Makers,
tin mice, 1930's . . . . . . $175.00 +

Car, Chrysler, Hubley,
iron $45.00-55.00

Monkey on a string,
1903 . . . . $40.00-50.00

Double decker bus, Arcade, cast
iron . . . . $200.00 +

Wind-up "GI Joe and his
Journeying Jeep", tin,
7" $15.00-25.00

Cap pistol, Columbia, 1880's,
iron $30.00-40.00

Stove, cast iron $35.00-45.00

Pull toy, rabbit on wheels,
"Bunny", tin $12.00-15.00

Sewing machine, iron, on
base $25.00-30.00

Fire wagon, ladders, team and
driver, iron, 1800's . . . $275.00 +

Pull toy, bear on wheels, soft,
Steiff . . . . $200.00 +

Rocking horse, wood with wood
rockers, carved . . . . . . $300.00 +

Wind-up, "Jazzbo Jim", banjo
player on roof, tin,
1920's . . . . $200.00 +

Noah's Ark, paper and wood,
1900's $20.00-25.00

Fire wagon, pumper, team and
driver, 1800's . . . . $275.00 +

Puzzle, wood and paper blocks,
1880's $70.00-80.00

Grasshopper, iron, Hubley,
1930's . . . . $200.00 +

Composition "witch" marionette, with her original broom. This pup- **pet is worth about $25.00-35.00.**

Paddlewheeler, iron,
Puritan $125.00-135.00
Windup, Ferris Wheel, "Hercules"
tin $75.00-85.00
Windmill, tin and wood,
21" tall $60.00-75.00
Miniature bookcase, 11"x9",
wood $150.00-175.00
Miniature spoon rack, punched
design, tin .... $200.00 +
Jumping jack, wood with pull
string, carved, painted,
early .... $300.00 +
Miniature hutch, 23"
tall, wood $200.00
Doll cradle, with posts, wood, early
1800's $200.00

Toy Soldiers

Toy soldiers of lead, wood, paper, iron, tin, pewter, or composition have become very popular among collectors. Military miniatures have always had an attraction for men and boys alike and even author Robert Louis Stevenson was an avid wargamer. Some of the most sought after toy soldiers are very detailed lead figures from England and those made of a wood-glue composition mixture from Germany in the 1930's. Lead casting sets for home use were sold in the 30's and 40's and they are also popular. Figures other than soldiers are collectible including bands, farm, Indians, cowboys, civilian, sports figures and others. Beware of reproduction soldiers molded in early shapes and styles.

"Soldiers on Parade", boxed set,
McLoughlin, 1890's,
paper $175.00-200.00
Baseball player, Auburn,
rubber $2.00-3.00
Nurse, Auburn, rubber . $2.00-3.00
Chinese infantryman, Barclay, lead,
1930's $5.00-7.50
Japanese officer, Barclay, lead,
1930's $7.00-10.00

World War II era sailors from a home casting set. These lead figures bring $1.00-2.00 each. The balsa amphibian from the same era is worth about $10.00-12.00.

260

German made figure of Hermann Goering, 3" tall. Worth about $75.00-100.00.

Ethiopian Chief, Grey Iron, 1930's
   lead $5.00-7.00
Boy Scout, Barclay, lead $5.00-7.00
Turkish soldiers, English set of 6,
   lead $75.00-100.00
Mounted Scots Band, Britains,
   14 pieces, lead .... $300.00.00 +
Wood soldiers, lithographed, set
   of 10 .... $100.00-120.00
Pirate Chief, Grey Iron,
   lead $4.00-5.00
Colonial soldier, mounted, lead,
   Grey Iron $4.00-5.00
Train Porter, Barclay, lead,
   black $6.00-8.00
Train Conductor, Barclay,
   lead $3.00-5.00
Black Prince, Courtenay, lead,
   1930's $65.00-75.00
Newsreel soldier, All-Nu, lead,
   early 1940's $30.00-32.50
Football player, All-Nu, lead,
   early 1940's $5.00-6.00

Paper soldiers from World War II, 25¢-75¢ each. Canvas tent, $10.00-12.00.

A Lionel locomotive and tender car in O gauge, made in the early 1940's. This engine and coal car would bring $15.00-25.00 from an interested collector.

Toy Trains

Toy trains combine the lure of the railroad with the appeal of childhood memories for many collectors. Most collectors are interested in the electric trains in standard gauges, but any toy train is popular. Wood and paper trains, tin, cast iron, clockwork, friction, steam or any combination is of interest to the toy train enthusiast. Though many train collectors want working examples most are more concerned with the outward appearance of the train. Lionel trains are by far the most collected in this country, and they bring reasonably good prices.

American Flyer #21130, engine and
   5 cars $65.00-70.00
Lionel "Hiawatha Steamer",
   1930's . . . . $250.00 +
American Flyer, "City of Denver"
   engine and 2 cars,
   1930's $125.00-150.00

Ives, O gauge #3255, engine and
   3 cars . . . . $250.00 +
American Flyer #3020, engine and
   3 cars . . . . $375.00 +
Lionel O gauge #1666, engine and
   4 cars . . . . $125.00 +
American Flyer #3110, engine and
   5 cars . . . . $275.00 +
Wood, hand carved, engine and
   3 cars, 1800's 23" . . . . $100.00 +
Ives, clockwork, 5 cars . . $200.00 +
Tin, Union Pacific,
   wind-up $20.00-25.00
Iron, engine and tender,
   1850's . . . . $200.00 +

Watches

Watches hold a fascination for many American collectors. There are hundreds of old watches available but generally, the most popular are those made by Waltham, Elgin, Illinois, Dueber-Hampton, Hamilton, Howard and Seth Thomas. Values given here are for watch movements and cases in good running condition.

Top Row, left to right:
Woman's English, 15 jewel, stem wind, stem set, silver, open face, Circa 1915 .... $30.00
Woman's Swiss movement, 7 jewel, 14K gold and enamel, open face, Circa 1900 .... $45.00
Woman's hunting case, Marcella Swiss, 15 jewel, stem wind, lever set, 14k gold, enamel dial, Circa 1905 .... $175.00
Woman's, English, 21 jewel, gold and enamel portrait, Circa 1900 .... $200.00
Woman's, 14k gold and enamel, 7 jewel, open face, stem wind, stem set, Circa 1900 .... $100.00
Woman's, 14k gold, Hampden, 7 jewel, stem wind, lever set, hunting case, Circa 1890 $200.00
Watch pin, heavy gold, sculptured and engraved, Circa 1900 . $75.00
Woman's, gold with "Pie Crust" engraved hunting case, Circa 1880 .... $325.00
Woman's, Elgin, 18k gold, 15 jewel, with "Pie Crust" engraved hunting case, stem wind, stem set, Circa 1897 .... $300.00
Chain with Slide, 14k gold with cabochon garnet, opal and pearls, slide with 52" 14k chain, Circa 1900 .... $250.00
Woman's, 14k gold hunting case, Molly Stark model, Hampden, 7 jewel, stem wind, stem set, Circa 1915 .... $175.00
Woman's oxidized silver case, open face, French, 10 jewel, stem wind, pin set, Circa 1890 .... $75.00
Woman's, Elgin, 15 jewel, hunting case, silver "Pie Crust", illustrated dial (stem set at 3 o'clock), Circa 1875 .... $100.00

Woman's 15 jewel, Swiss, 14k case, open face, Circa 1915 .... $75.00
Man's grosgrain watch fob, low karat gold, engraved pendant, set with 3 rubies, Circa 1910 .... $25.00
Man's grosgrain watch fob, gold engraved, double-hasp buckle, Circa 1920 .... $20.00
Man's double case, 10 jewel silver, open face, French hand-painted porcelain dial with oxidized metal protective case, Circa 1850 .... $150.00
Man's double-case Swiss, 10 jewel, open face, silver stem wind, pin set, in protective case, Circa 1890 .... $100.00
Man's, English, 10 jewel, open face, engraved 18k gold, key wind and key set with key, Circa 1870 .... $275.00
Man's, Elgin, stem wind, stem set, 7 jewel, hunting case, 14k gold, Circa 1879 .... $225.00
Man's, hunting case, 17 jewel, 14k gold, French, stem wind, lever set, Circa 1900 .... $225.00
Man's, Elgin, 7 jewel, hunting case, 14k gold, stem wind, stem set, Circa 1870 .... $250.00
Man's/woman's, 7 jewel, Elgin, hunting case, 14k gold, stem set, Circa 1890 .... $275.00
Man's/woman's 7 jewel, Waltham, 14k gold, hunting case, stem wind, stem set, Circa 1900 .... $275.00
Man's/woman's, 7 jewel, 14k gold, hunting case, Seth Thomas, stem wind, stem set, Circa 1884 .... $350.00
Man's/woman's, 15 jewel, 18k gold, Waltham, hunting case, Circa 1890 .... $200.00
Man's/woman's, 15 jewel, 14k gold, Elgin, hunting case, stem wind, stem set, Circa 1879 .... $250.00

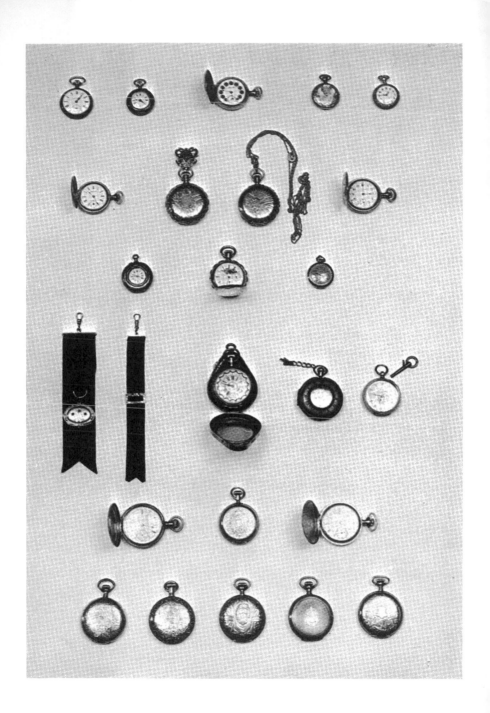

Watch Fobs

A watch fob is a weighted piece at the end of a watch chain or strap. They were both attractive and useful and were quite common from the late 1800's until shortly after World War I. They are usually made of brass, cast iron, bronze, copper or celluloid and are generally political, advertising or railroad in nature. Most are quite attractive and creative in design and because of their relatively small size can be displayed and transported easily. The collector should be cautious in purchasing watch fobs because many are being reproduced today.

Keen Kutter, 1910.... $15.00-17.00

Red Goose Shoes,
  1912 .... $17.00-20.00
Caterpillar, 1940's $8.00-10.00
Mack Truck, bulldog,
  1960's $5.00-10.00
Studebaker, 1930's ... $27.50-32.50
Buick, enameled, 1920 $30.00-35.00
Union Brewing Co.,
  1900's............ $25.00-30.00
Kelloggs Corn Flakes . $20.00-25.00
Hires Root Beer $40.00-45.00
John Deere $35.00-50.00
Old Dutch Cleanser .. $12.00-17.00
Dr. Pepper $40.00-50.00
Coca Cola, girl with
  bottle .... $100.00+
Allis Chalmers $10.00-12.00
Pepsi Cola $55.00-65.00

A selection of watch fobs.

Weathervanes

Weathervanes, placed on rooftops of houses or barns were used as decoration and as an indication of wind strength and direction. Weathervanes have been made in a variety of metals, but the most valuable and popular seems to be copper. Collectors should beware of reproductions, because many early styles are being reproduced today.

Cow, copper .... $750.00 +
Horse, copper, walking $1000.00 +
Horse & jockey, copper $1500.00 +
Dog, copper .... $750.00 +

This handmade sheet metal weather-vane is from Maine and worth about $1400.00.

Eagle, copper . . . . $500.00 +
Horse, trotting,
   cast iron . . . . $300.00 +
Horse, standing,
   sheet metal . . . . $100.00 +
Rooster, zinc . . . . $300.00 +
Squirrel, iron, flat . . . . . . $250.00 +
Cow, iron . . . . $300.00 +

Weller Pottery

Weller is another American pottery that made art pottery as well as inexpensive decorative pieces. Naturally the more elaborate art pieces bring the highest prices, but the less expensive pieces are being collected as well.

Weller art pottery. Aurelian vase, 18" signed, $1500.00 + ; Corleone vase, 17" signed, $500.00 + ; silver overlay Aurelian vase, 11½" signed, $1000.00 + .

**Weller Dickensware. Top row: 11"
signed tankard $2000.00; 12"
tankard $2000.00; bottom row: 13"
vase $2000.00; 13" vase $700.00.**

Weller Lamar: vases, $100.00;
lamp, $300.00.

Weller Brighton birds. Bluebird, $170.00-200.00; woodpecker. $75.00-100.00; pheasant, $250.00- 300.00; 7½'' parrot, $170.00-200.00; large parrots, 200.00-300.00.

Vase, Lonhuda, 4½",
  signed $170.00-200.00
Vase, Louwelsa, 7",
  signed $85.00-110.00
Lamp, Aurelian, 27",
  signed .... $1000.00+
Mug, 6", Turada .. $210.00-250.00
Pillow vase, Dickensware,
  portrait, 7" .... $1500.00+
Vase, 16", Dickensware, Don
  Quizote, signed ..... $1500.00+
Tobacco jar, Dickensware, skull,
  5½" .... $1000.00+
Flash vase, Eocean, 7½",
  signed .... $600.00+
Vase, Etna, frog and snake
  in relief $165.00-175.00
Hanging parrot, 15".... $250.00+
Fishing boy in boat,
  Muskota $100.00-125.00
Monkey on Peanut,
  novelty $35.00-45.00
Vase, 6", Stellar $75.00-90.00
Triple candleholder, wild
  rose .... pair $40.00-50.00
Vase, 6", Rudlor $20.00-25.00

Western Collectibles

The old west holds a fascination for many collectors. Holsters, gunbelts, cowboy equipment, guns, photography, express company collectibles or memorabilia connected with cowboys, outlaws, lawmen or the western United States in the nineteenth century is collectible. Be very careful to avoid reproductions and fakes in this area.

Treasure box, Wells Fargo, wood
  and iron, 1890's ...... $750.00+
Photograph, cowboy,
  1880's $60.00-70.00
Hat, conductor style, Wells Fargo
  aluminum badge,
  1900-1910 ...... $150.00-200.00
Hat, conductor style, Wells Fargo
  nickled brass badge,
  1900-1910 ...... $200.00-250.00
Saddlebag holster, Main and
  Winchester, for Colt Navy
  revolver, leather ... $300.00 pair

A pair of shop-made spurs worth about $165.00-185.00.

A Mexican made holster for a single action , $75.00-95.00

Spurs, embossed leather, eagle
mounts, Kelly brand . . $225.00 +
Chaps, batwing style,
leather $175.00-225.00
Chaps, black angora
wooly . . . . $350.00 +
Push dagger with sheath . . . $200.00
Sign, Wells Fargo & Co., wood,
6' long $750.00

Handcuffs, early
type $75.00-100.00
Saloon cigar lighter, bronze slave
head mounted on claw, late
1800's . . . . $350.00 +
Poster, Buffalo Bills Wild West
Show, 20''x30'',
1891 . . . . $200.00 +
Annie Oakley signature and
photo . . . . $100.00 +

Wicker

Wicker was first imported into the United States from the Orient in the 18th Century. By the middle of the 1800's, it was being manufactured in America. Elaborate styles were popular at first, followed by a plainer design. Naturally the older pieces are more valuable than the more recently produced wicker. The collector should take caution when buying wicker because many pieces are being manufactured today. A good general rule of thumb in determining the age of wicker is to study the thickness of the weave. Before 1900 the reed was of a light quality and woven very close. After 1900 a heavier reed with a loose weaving pattern came into use.

Working batwing chaps like these usually bring between $175.00 and $225.00.

A wicker rocker worth about $125.00.

Straight chair	$100.00-125.00
Davenport	$250.00-350.00
Hamper	$20.00-35.00
Straight, fireside chair	$200.00.00+
Lounge	$250.00.00+
Rocking chair	$85.00-125.00
Tea cart	$200.00+
Baby buggy	$85.00-125.00
Library table	$90.00-115.00
Planter	$85.00-95.00
Round table	$150.00-175.00
Settee	$200.00-250.00
Footstool	$25.00-30.00

An early wicker birdcage valued at about $50.00.

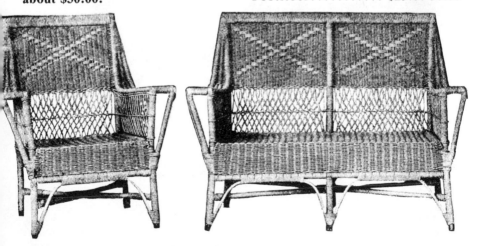

This wicker armchair and settee would bring $300.00 or more today.

World's Fair & Exposition Collectibles

World's Fairs and Expositions held in this country have provided collectors with many souvenirs, giveaways, and commemorative items connected with the events. These items are made of wood, glass, paper, metal, in a wide variety of categories.

1939 New York World's Fair, ceramic vase, Lenox .. $200.00 +

1893 World's Columbian Exposition, fan ...... $100.00 +

1893 World's Columbian Exposition, poster $300.00

1876 Centennial Exhibition, map of grounds ... $15.00-20.00

1876 Centennial Exhibition, salt shaker, Liberty Bell $60.00-70.00

1904 St. Louis World's Fair, spoon, silver & goldwash .. $30.00-40.00

1904 St. Louis World's Fair, map $8.00-10.00

1933 Chicago World's Fair, ashtray, Century of Progress.......... $15.00-20.00

1933 Chicago World's Fair, A&P advertising token ... $5.00-10.00

1939 New York World's Fair, ball & sphere, metal . $8.00-10.00

1893 World's Columbian Exposition, stoneware pitcher, Washington .... $275.00 +

1901 Pan American Exhibition, ceramic mug $35.00-40.00

1901 Pan American Exhibition, stickpin "To Unite the Americas" $20.00-25.00

1893 World's Columbian Exposition, admission ticket, Lincoln $7.00-10.00

1876 Centennial Exhibition, paperweight, anvil . $12.00-15.00

1933 Chicago World's Fair, cigarette case, nickel plated $12.00-15.00

1876 Centennial Exhibition, silk ribbon, Memorial Hall $25.00-30.00

1904 St. Louis World's Fair, paperweight U.S. Government bldg. . $15.00-20.00

1876 Centennial Exhibition, paper & silk fan ... $75.00-85.00

Buttons from the 1933 and 1939 World's Fairs, $3.00-5.00 each.

A photograph of the Ferris wheel at   1893, $10.00.
the World's Columbian Exposition,

For more extensive information on the subjects included in the *Flea Market Trader* the following books offer illustrations and current values. The books below are currently in print and may be purchased at leading bookstores or ordered direct from Collector Books, P.O. Box 3009, Paducah, KY 42001. Please add $1.00 for postage and handling.

ADVERTISING CARDS
Advertising Cards, Jim & Cathy McQuary 5.95

ADVERTISING COLLECTIBLES
Old Advertising, Jim Cope . . . 9.95

ADVERTISING DOLLS
Advertising Dolls, Joleen Robison & Kay Sellers 9.95

AKRO AGATE GLASSWARE
Encyclopedia of Akro Agate Glass, Gene Florence 8.95

AUTOGRAPHS
Paper Collectibles, Robert Connoly 9.95

AVON
Hastins Avon Encyclopedia, Bud Hastin 18.95

BANKS
Collecting Toys, Books Americana 9.95

Collector's Encyclopedia of Toys & Banks, Don Cranmer 9.95

BARBED WIRE
Collector's Encyclopedia of Barbed Wire, Col. R.J. Thurgood . . 3.95

BARBIE
Collector's Encyclopedia of Barbie Dolls, Sybil DeWein & Joan Ashabraner 17.95

BEER CANS
American Beer Can Encyclopedia, Thomas Toepfer 7.95

BLUE & WHITE POTTERY
Blue & White Stoneware Pottery, Crockery, Edith Harbin 7.95

BLUE RIDGE
Blue Ridge Dinnerware, Bill & Betty Newbound 9.95

BOTTLES
Bottle Pricing Guide, Hugh Cleveland 7.95

BUTTER MOLDS
Butter Molds, Jim Trice 7.95

CARNIVAL GLASS
Millersburg, Queen of Carnival Glass, Bill Edwards 8.95

Imperial Carnival Glass, Bill
Edwards 9.95

Northwood, King of Carnival
Glass, Bill Edwards 8.95

Rarities in Carnival Glass, Bill
Edwards 8.95

CHILDREN'S DISHES
Children's Glass Dishes, Doris
Lechler & Virginia O'Neill . 11.95

CLOCKS
Standard Antique Clock Value
Guide, Alex Wescott 11.95

CUT GLASS
The Standard Cut Glass Value
Guide, Jo Evers 8.95

COCA-COLA COLLECTIBLES
Old Advertising, Jim Cope ... 9.95

The Standard Antique Doll Identification & Value Guide ... 7.95

Kestner, Simon & Halbig Dolls,
Patricia R, Smith 7.95

The Standard Modern Doll Identification & Value Guide ... 7.95

Modern Collector's Dolls I,
Patricia R. Smith 17.95

Modern Collector's Dolls, II,
Patricia R. Smith 17.95

Modern Collector's Dolls III,
Patricia R. Smith 17.95

Shirley Temple Dolls & Collectibles, Patricia R. Smith ... 17.95

Teen Dolls Identification & Value
Guide, Patricia R. Smith ... 7.95

Collector's Encyclopedia of
Barbie Dolls, Sybil DeWein &
Joan Ashabraner 17.95

Patricia Smith's Doll Values, Antique to Modern, Patricia R.
Smith 8.95

Madame Alexander Collector's
Dolls, Patricia R. Smith ... 19.95

DEPRESSION GLASS
Pocket Guide to Depression Glass,
Gene Florence 8.95

The Collector's Encyclopedia of
Depression Glass, Gene
Florence 14.95

DOLLHOUSES
Dollhouses Past & Present, Don &
Helen Mitchell 9.95

DOLLS
Antique Collector's Dolls I,
Patricia R. Smith 17.95
Antique Collector's Dolls II,
Patricia R. Smith 17.95

FIESTA
The Collector's Encyclopedia of
Fiesta, Sharon & Bob
Huxford 8.95

FOUNTAIN PENS
Fountain Pens, History, Repair &
Current Values, Cliff
Lawrence 7.95

FRENCH DOLLS
French Dolls,
Patricia R. Smith 8.95

FRUIT JARS
1000 Fruit Jars, Bill Schroeder 4.95
The Red Book of Fruit Jars, Alice
M. Creswick 11.95

GERMAN DOLLS
German Dolls,
Patricia R. Smith 8.95

GLASS CANDLESTICKS
Glass Candlesticks I, Margaret &
Douglas Archer 8.95
Glass Candelsticks II, Margaret &
Douglas Archer 8.95

GRANITEWARE
Graniteware, Fred & Rose
Booher 7.95

GUNS
Modern Guns, Russell & Steve
Quertermous 11.95

HALF-DOLLS
China Half-Figures Called Pin-
cushion Dolls, Frieda
Marion 7.95

The Collector's Encyclopedia of
Half- Dolls, Frieda Marion &
Norma Werner 29.95

HATPINS
The Collector's Encyclopedia of
Hatpins & Hatpin Holders,
Lillian Baker 19.95

HUMMEL
Hummel Figurines, Carl F.
Luckey 9.95

INDIAN ARTIFACTS
Indian Artifacts, Lar Hothem 9.95

INSULATORS
800 Insulators, Bill Schroeder 3.95

JEWELRY
100 Years of Collectible Jewelry,
Lillian Baker 8.95

KESTNER DOLLS
Kestner and Simon & Halbig Dolls,
Patricia R. Smith 7.95

KITCHEN COLLECTIBLES
Collector's Guide to Kitchen Anti-
ques, Don &
Carol Raycraft 17.95

LIMOGES
The Collector's Encyclopedia of
Limoges Porcelain, Mary Frank
Gaston 19.95

LOCKS
Collectible Locks, Richard
Holiner 5.95

MADAME ALEXANDER DOLLS
Madame Alexander Collector's
Dolls, Patricia R. Smith . . . 19.95

McCOY POTTERY
The Collector's Encyclopedia of McCoy Pottery, Sharon & Bob Huxford 17.95

NAZI COLLECTIBLES
German Military Collectibles, Robert McCarthy 6.95

NIPPON
The Collector's Encyclopedia of Nipppon, Joan Van Patten 19.95

OAK
Marketplace Guide to Oak Furniture, Peter Blundell 17.95

Value Guide to Oak Furniture, Con over Hill 7.95

OCCUPIED JAPAN
Occupied Japan Collectibles, Gene Florence 12.95

OLD WEST
Old West Antiques & Collectibles 22.95

ORIENTAL DOLLS
Oriental Dolls, Patricia R. Smith 9.95

PAPER COLLECTIBLES
Paper Collectibles, Robert Connolly 9.95

PAPER DOLLS
Collector's Guide to Paper Dolls, Mary Young 9.95

PRIMITIVES
Primitives, Our Handmade Heritage, Catherine Thuro 17.95
Primitives, Our American Heritage, Kathryn McNerney 8.95

RAZORS
Straight Razor Collecting, Robert Doyle 7.95

RECORDS
American Premium Record Guide, Les Docks 9.95

SHAWNEE POTTERY
Shawnee Pottery, Dolores Simon 7.95

SHEET MUSIC
Introducing the Song Sheet, Helen Westin 14.95

SHIRLEY TEMPLE
Shirley Temple Dolls & Collectibles, Patricia R. Smith ... 17.95

SIMON & HALBIG
Kestner and Simon & Halbig Dolls, Patricia R. Smith 7.95

TOOLS
Antique Tools, Our American
  Heritage,
  Kathryn McNerney 8.95

TOYS & TOY SOLDIERS
Collecting Toys, Books
  Americana 9.95

Collector's Encyclopdeia of Toys &
  Banks, Don Cranmer 9.95

WELLER
The Collector's Encyclopdeia of
  Weller Pottery, Bob & Sharon
  Huxford 24.95

Illustration Acknowledgements

INDEX